How Should America Respond to Illegal Immigration?

Hal Marcovitz

INCONTROVERSY

ReferencePoint
Press®

San Diego, CA

© 2012 ReferencePoint Press, Inc.
Printed in the United States

For more information, contact:
ReferencePoint Press, Inc.
PO Box 27779
San Diego, CA 92198
www. ReferencePointPress.com

Picture Credits:
AP Images: 54, 63
© Bettmann/Corbis: 17, 20
© Bradley C. Bower/Corbis: 40
© Rick D'Elia/Corbis: 47
© Kevin Flaming/Corbis: 7
© Christopher Morris/Corbis: 31
© Tim Shaffer/Reuters/Corbis: 69
© Jeff Topping/Reuters/Corbis: 74
© Underwood & Underwood/Corbis: 35

LIBRARY OF CONGRESS CATALOGING-IN-PUBLICATION DATA

Marcovitz, Hal.
  How should America respond to illegal immigration? / by Hal Marcovitz.
    p. cm. — (In controversy series)
  Includes bibliographical references and index.
  ISBN-13: 978-1-60152-173-6 (hardback)
  ISBN-10: 1-60152-173-1 (hardback)
  1. Illegal aliens—United States. 2. Illegal aliens—Government policy—United States. 3. United States—Emigration and immigration—Government policy. I. Title.
  JV6483.M296 2011
  325.73—dc22
                                                                              2011004163

Contents

Foreword

In 2008, as the U.S. economy and economies worldwide were falling into the worst recession since the Great Depression, most Americans had difficulty comprehending the complexity, magnitude, and scope of what was happening. As is often the case with a complex, controversial issue such as this historic global economic recession, looking at the problem as a whole can be overwhelming and often does not lead to understanding. One way to better comprehend such a large issue or event is to break it into smaller parts. The intricacies of global economic recession may be difficult to understand, but one can gain insight by instead beginning with an individual contributing factor such as the real estate market. When examined through a narrower lens, complex issues become clearer and easier to evaluate.

This is the idea behind ReferencePoint Press's *In Controversy* series. The series examines the complex, controversial issues of the day by breaking them into smaller pieces. Rather than looking at the stem cell research debate as a whole, a title would examine an important aspect of the debate such as *Is Stem Cell Research Necessary?* or *Is Embryonic Stem Cell Research Ethical?* By studying the central issues of the debate individually, researchers gain a more solid and focused understanding of the topic as a whole.

Each book in the series provides a clear, insightful discussion of the issues, integrating facts and a variety of contrasting opinions for a solid, balanced perspective. Personal accounts and direct quotes from academic and professional experts, advocacy groups, politicians, and others enhance the narrative. Sidebars add depth to the discussion by expanding on important ideas and events. For quick reference, a list of key facts concludes every chapter. Source notes, an annotated organizations list, bibliography, and index provide student researchers with additional tools for papers and class discussion.

The *In Controversy* series also challenges students to think critically about issues, to improve their problem-solving skills, and to sharpen their ability to form educated opinions. As President Barack Obama stated in a March 2009 speech, success in the twenty-first century will not be measurable merely by students' ability to "fill in a bubble on a test but whether they possess 21st century skills like problem-solving and critical thinking and entrepreneurship and creativity." Those who possess these skills will have a strong foundation for whatever lies ahead.

No one can know for certain what sort of world awaits today's students. What we can assume, however, is that those who are inquisitive about a wide range of issues; open-minded to divergent views; aware of bias and opinion; and able to reason, reflect, and reconsider will be best prepared for the future. As the international development organization Oxfam notes, "Today's young people will grow up to be the citizens of the future: but what that future holds for them is uncertain. We can be quite confident, however, that they will be faced with decisions about a wide range of issues on which people have differing, contradictory views. If they are to develop as global citizens all young people should have the opportunity to engage with these controversial issues."

In Controversy helps today's students better prepare for tomorrow. An understanding of the complex issues that drive our world and the ability to think critically about them are essential components of contributing, competing, and succeeding in the twenty-first century.

A Country Divided

When he was 19 years old Alfredo Quiñones-Hinojosa hoped to escape the poverty that gripped his hometown of Mexicali, a city in Mexico just across the border from California. And so one night in 1987, Quiñones-Hinojosa scaled a chain-link border fence, slipping into America in search of a new start. "My original plan, just like many people who come to the United States, was to make a lot of money and come back to my country," he says. "It took me about a year to realize that was a false dream."[1]

For the next three years, Quiñones-Hinojosa worked as a farm laborer, picking vegetables in the fields near Fresno, California. It was a grim existence—home was a ramshackle camper. Very often, the only food Quiñones-Hinojosa could obtain was the food he picked in the fields—tomatoes, corn, and broccoli. "I ate what I was picking," he says. "I wore the same pair of jeans the whole year."[2] At first he spoke no English, but kept an English-language dictionary in his pocket and studied constantly. Soon he was fluent in English and, now with a little money saved, was able to move into a small apartment. He also found a better job as a welder in a railroad yard. At night, Quiñones-Hinojosa took classes at San Joaquin Delta College.

Winning His Green Card

Quiñones-Hinojosa eventually won legal status. He took advantage of an amnesty program that had been established by the federal government, granting residency visas, also known as green cards, to illegal immigrants who could prove they had been working regularly. After receiving his green card, Quiñones-Hinojosa married, graduated from the University of California at Berkeley, and enrolled at Harvard Medical School in Massachusetts. Quiñones-Hinojosa would go on to graduate from Harvard, where he would also deliver the commencement address. Today, Quiñones-Hinojosa is a brain surgeon at Johns Hopkins University Hospital in Maryland. He is also a US citizen, having been naturalized in 1997.

The story of Quiñones-Hinojosa illustrates that many illegal immigrants have the potential to make contributions to American society. On the other hand, many do not. Some, for example, have been identified as drug dealers and other violent criminals. Unlike Quiñones-Hinojosa and other hardworking immigrants who seldom earn headlines, those who come here illegally and then break other laws are the ones who receive media attention.

National Debate

It is believed that there are more than 11 million illegal immigrants living in the United States. Their status as illegal residents has sparked a divisive national debate among Americans, many of whom are passionate in their beliefs.

On one side of the issue stand people who firmly believe that the government should round up all illegal immigrants and send them back to their countries of origin. "The dam is breaking," says William Gheen, president of the Raleigh, North Carolina–based

Migrant workers hoist buckets filled with tomatoes onto their shoulders during Florida's harvest season. For migrant workers and others who enter the United States illegally, the risk of harm or capture is worth the chance of a better life.

Americans for Legal Immigration. "[Illegal immigration] is having a degrading effect on wages and other quality-of-life issues like community health and community safety."[3]

Moreover, Gheen and other critics believe that America's southern border should be patrolled relentlessly and that perhaps even an impenetrable fence should be erected along the country's 1,950-mile border (3,140km) with Mexico. Says conservative columnist Sam Francis, "The fact is that a nation penetrated every year by some 300,000 illegal aliens and in which some 11 million illegal aliens live permanently is not a nation experiencing 'immigration.' It is a nation experiencing invasion and conquest."[4]

On the other side of the issue stand an equally passionate group of Americans who believe that strict anti-immigration policies would never work: that no matter how much the border was patrolled or how high a fence might be erected, immigrants with a need and desire would find a way to enter the country. Moreover, many people believe that harsh measures against immigrants (even those who enter the country illegally) run counter to one of the principles on which the country is founded—that all people, especially those seeking new and better lives, should be welcomed within American borders. "Are not these men and women exactly like us?" asks David DeCosse, director of campus ethics programs at Santa Clara University in California. "In asking this question, it becomes possible to see undocumented immigrants as more than violators of a law and deserving of deportation. Instead they emerge as fellow human beings, who have sometimes endured great hardship to seek a better life here, much as our ancestors did."[5]

No Middle Ground

DeCosse and other advocates urge American lawmakers to adopt a path through which illegal immigrants can attain citizenship. However, lawmakers stand divided on the issue and there does not appear to be a middle ground. Indeed, recent efforts to find compromise have fallen short in Washington, DC, as well as in many state capitals. Some stern anti-immigration measures adopted by

"The dam is breaking. [Illegal immigration] is having a degrading effect on wages and other quality-of-life issues like community health and community safety."[3]

— William Gheen, president of Americans for Legal Immigration.

state governments have been challenged in the courts, where the cases are likely to remain bottled up for years to come.

Following the amnesty that granted legal residency to Quiñones-Hinojosa, the federal government has approved other amnesties that have provided legal status to thousands of people who entered the country illegally. However, those programs have been sporadic and brief—there is no firm amnesty policy in America.

Quiñones-Hinojosa says that it is clear to him that current immigration policies are ineffective. He says that as long as poverty, despair, and political turmoil exist in other countries, people will look toward America as a haven. "I know what it was that drove me to jump the fence," he says. "It was poverty and frustration with a system that would have never allowed me to be who I am today. As long as there is poverty in the rest of the world and we export our culture through movies and television, people who are hungry are going to come here. There's no way to stop it."[6]

Illegal immigrants continue to pour into the United States while authorities make use of a smorgasbord of mostly ineffective existing laws to find illegal visitors and either send them home or, in limited cases, grant them legal residency. In the present legislative climate, with neither side inclined to agree to meaningful compromise, replacement of the ineffective measures does not seem likely soon.

> "It becomes possible to see undocumented immigrants as more than violators of a law and deserving of deportation. Instead they emerge as fellow human beings, who have sometimes endured great hardship to seek a better life here, much as our ancestors did."[5]
>
> — David DeCosse, director of campus ethics programs at Santa Clara University.

Facts

- **Sixty-eight percent of respondents to a 2010 Gallup Organization poll called halting the flow of illegal immigration into the United States either "extremely important" or "very important."**

- **The size of the illegal immigration population of America has more than tripled since 1990, when the Pew Hispanic Center estimated that about 3.5 million illegal immigrants were living in the United States.**

What Are the Roots of the Controversy over Illegal Immigration?

Rob Krentz's family had ranched in the San Bernardino Valley region of southern Arizona for generations, so Krentz was well familiar with all the canyons, paths, and back roads of the remote scrubland just north of the Mexican border. In recent years, though, whenever Krentz ventured into the desert, he always took a gun because of the likelihood that he would encounter illegal immigrants from Mexico making their way into Arizona.

Although Krentz did not fear most of the immigrants he encountered, he knew that some of them carried drugs into the country, acting as couriers for notorious Mexican drug cartels. Very often, gangs of Mexican bandits known as "rip crews," or "*bajadores*," prey on these hapless travelers, murdering them for the drugs hidden on their bodies or what little cash or other valuables they might be carrying. Krentz was aware that encountering a band of *bajadores* could be dangerous. "You never know who you're dealing with out here because you get all kinds of traffic through here,"[7] said William McDonald, another Arizona rancher.

When Krentz did not return home on March 27, 2010, his family notified authorities. After searching the region for several hours, a police helicopter spotted the missing man's body. He had been shot to death in a remote canyon about 20 miles (32km) north of the Mexican border. Police were able to track the killer's footprints south toward the border—meaning that whoever killed Krentz is likely to have entered the United States illegally, killed the rancher, and returned to Mexico. Police have never caught the killer—they don't know whether the rancher was murdered by *bajadores* or simply by a solitary person, probably a Latino without papers, who had feared that Krentz would turn him over to US Border Patrol agents.

Days after Krentz's body was found, his family issued this statement to reporters:

> We hold no malice towards the Mexican people for this senseless act but do hold the political forces in this country and Mexico accountable for what has happened. Their disregard of our repeated pleas and warnings of impending violence towards our community fell on deaf ears shrouded in political correctness. As a result, we have paid the ultimate price for their negligence in credibly securing our borderlands.[8]

Drug Trafficking and Illegal Immigration

The Krentz family's complaint illustrates the basic flaw that has plagued American immigration policy for more than a century: the US government has failed to develop an effective strategy for stemming the flow of people who enter the country illegally. Certainly, there have been many laws established regulating immigration and they do serve their purposes to a degree—enabling students, businesspeople, family members of US residents, and others to enter the country legally. Some laws contain provisions under which many visitors can eventually win American citizenship.

None of those laws has much meaning, though, to a poverty-stricken Mexican, Honduran, or Salvadoran who is willing to make a hazardous desert crossing. Once in the United States, the typical illegal immigrant hopes to live beneath the radar of American law so that he or she can eke out a living in America doing the most menial labor—often as a vegetable picker, gardener, or housekeeper.

Critics of American immigration policy contend that illegal immigrants are responsible for a host of ills and social problems. They point toward the violence and drug trafficking that often accompanies immigrants as they make the crossing—a circumstance they contend is well illustrated by the Krentz murder. "What we see in drug trafficking, particularly down in Mexico, is a level of violence unheard of here," says Risa Vetri Ferman, the district attorney of Montgomery County, Pennsylvania. "And when we see people or drug dealers with those connections operating in our community, we want to nip that in the bud. We want to do everything we can to prevent that kind of violence from touching our community."[9] Ferman made those comments shortly after police in Montgomery County, which is located some 2,000 miles (3,220km) from the Mexican border, announced the arrests of seven people on drug trafficking charges. Of the seven people arrested, police identified six as illegal immigrants from Mexico.

Drug War in Mexico

The drugs that find their way to places like Montgomery County often originate in Central and South America. All those drugs move northward, across the US border, to be sold in cities, suburbs, and rural communities. With billions of dollars in illegal profits at stake, violence often breaks out among the gangs that seek to control the narcotics trade. In recent years the violence of the drug war has hit Mexico hard, particularly in the country's border cities.

In Ciudad Juárez, a Mexican city across the border from El Paso, Texas, drug gangs compete for turf. Gun battles, murders, and kidnappings have become common occurrences in Ciudad Juárez. To escape the violence, many residents have fled the city—since 2008, as many as 230,000 people are estimated to have left Ciudad Juárez, which formally had a population of some 1.4 million people. Said one 50-year-old businessman who spoke with a reporter, "It's a city that's dying. It's out of control."[10]

Health Care, Education, and Jobs

Many American authorities are convinced that many of the people fleeing the drug violence in Ciudad Juárez have traveled north, finding havens in El Paso and other American cities. These immigrants are generally not criminals—they are leaving their homes in fear for their lives. Most of them do not pose a threat to the safety of the American people; yet critics insist that they represent a burden on American society because of the way many live: homeless, unemployed, paying no federal taxes, and often as single mothers.

For example, under federal law no hospital emergency room in America is permitted to turn away a patient in need—all must be treated, no questions asked, regardless of ability to pay. Critics of illegal immigration contend that the law has given millions of illegal immigrants access to free health care, which is subsidized by taxpayers as well as everyone who pays medical bills. The anti-immigration group Federation for American Immigration Reform (FAIR) estimates the cost of providing free medical care to illegal immigrants at more than $1 billion a year. "Federal laws requiring hospitals to treat anyone who enters an emergency room regardless of ability to pay have created an unfunded mandate for states and localities to fund health care for . . . illegal aliens," says a report by FAIR. "Yet at the same time, lack of enforcement of federal laws against illegal immigration has led to a pool of nine to eleven million illegal aliens in the U.S.—and state and local taxpayers are being forced to foot the bill."[11]

Critics also contend that illegal immigrants take jobs from Americans. That view is held by Latrina Shields, an unemployed woman from Gainesville, Georgia, who has not been able to find work in any of the city's many poultry processing plants. "We can't find work because of them, and I'm not being racist," said Shields, who was interviewed by a reporter as she entered an unemployment office in Gainesville. "You see them in all the poultry jobs. They're everywhere."[12]

Most Illegal Immigrants Live Quietly

Although it may appear to workers like Latrina Shields that immigrants take jobs from Americans, others question whether this is the case. Many experts suggest that illegal immigrants are taking jobs that most Americans avoid—those that are the lowest paying and most menial. In fact, in 2010 a joint study by the University of California–Davis and Bocconi University in Italy suggested that without immigrant workers, many American companies would move their operations to countries where wages are lower. These moves would actually cost American jobs, since the companies at risk of closing their US facilities employ the legal US residents in higher-paid positions as well.

As for crime, critics point to many cases of criminal activity and violence sparked by illegal immigrants. Others, however, believe that the vast majority of illegal immigrants obey American laws. They reason that illegal immigrants seek only to live peaceful lives without drawing attention to themselves, since if they are arrested they are likely to be jailed and then deported. A 2007 study by the American Immigration Council of Washington, DC, found that American-born men between the ages of 18 and 39 are five times more likely to be incarcerated than foreign-born men in the same age group.

"We can't find work because of them, and I'm not being racist. You see them in all the poultry jobs. They're everywhere."[12]

— Latrina Shields, an unemployed woman from Gainesville, Georgia.

The Chinese Exclusion Act

Still, complaints like those voiced by Shields carry a familiar message—similar complaints about immigrants have been heard for more than a century. Fears that immigrants were stealing jobs from Americans were at the root of the first national law aimed at clamping down on immigration. That measure was the Chinese Exclusion Act, and it was signed into law in 1882 by President Chester A. Arthur.

Prior to adoption of the measure, there were virtually no restraints on immigration to America. Anybody who could afford passage could enter the country and millions did—coming not only from China and other Asian countries but from the many

The Braceros

The bracero program was intended to provide labor to American farms during World War II, but the Mexican government endorsed the program for another reason: officials hoped the program would help curb abuses faced by Mexican citizens who were desperate enough to use illegal methods of finding a new homeland.

The first bracero program was initiated in 1942. According to an agreement with Mexico, braceros were guaranteed minimum wages, clean living conditions, and transportation home. From 1942 until 1948, as many as 50,000 braceros a year found jobs in America. Others crossed the border illegally looking for work, however, and most did not receive the protections guaranteed under the agreement with Mexico.

In 1949 a second bracero agreement was signed. Under this agreement, 150,000 Mexicans who had previously crossed illegally were declared legal guest workers, meaning they were now eligible for the rights guaranteed to the braceros. This plan did not work, either. After the declaration of legal status for the illegal immigrants, thousands more flocked into the country; most received very low wages and lived in squalid conditions. The bracero program was shelved in 1965. By then some 300,000 illegal immigrants were entering the country each year, and many were paid very low wages at the farms where they found work.

European nations as well as Canada and Mexico. Prior to adoption of the Chinese Exclusion Act, America's borders were open wide to immigration, so virtually no one had to resort to illegal means to get in.

Indeed, more than a century before Congress adopted the Chinese Exclusion Act, Thomas Jefferson set the tone for the nation's attitude toward immigration when he stated his belief that it is the right of every human being to immigrate to the country of his or her choice:

> Our ancestors possessed a right, which nature has given to all men, of departing from the country in which chance, not choice, has placed them, of going in quest of new habitations, and of there establishing new societies, under such laws and regulations as, to them, shall seem most likely to promote public happiness.[13]

When Jefferson wrote those words he did not foresee the grim economic conditions that would much later burden poor Irish American factory workers in San Francisco. For years, the workers had griped about poor wages. But in 1870 they went on strike, demanding a raise in pay from $3 a day to $4 a day. The factory bosses responded not by granting concessions to the workers but by giving the jobs to Chinese immigrants who were willing to work for a mere $1 a day.

Violence and Ridicule

Losing their jobs to Chinese laborers hardly endeared the Chinese immigrants to Californians and others. In fact, the Chinese became the objects of scorn, violence, and ridicule. A poem, titled "The Heathen Chinee," which accused the Chinese of not only taking American jobs but cheating at cards, received wide circulation when it was published in the newspapers of the era. In 1877 emotions reached a fever pitch when 10,000 white San Franciscans rioted, burning homes and businesses in the city's Chinatown neighborhood. Four Chinese immigrants were killed in the chaos.

Demands for politicians in Washington, DC, to take official action against the Chinese bore fruit in 1882, when the Chinese Exclusion Act banned most Chinese immigration for 10 years, with exceptions for merchants, students, and teachers only. The act was renewed as it was about to expire, then made permanent in 1904. The Chinese Exclusion Act would not be repealed until 1943, the year Congress lifted the restrictions as a gesture to the Chinese government, which had been enlisted as an American ally

in World War II. (Although Congress repealed the measure, law-makers passed a subsequent act restricting Chinese immigration to America to a mere 105 persons a year.)

The Chinese Exclusion Act was effective: in the 40 years following adoption of the law, the population of Chinese-born residents in America dropped from more than 100,000 to less than 65,000. Relatively few Chinese immigrants were able to set foot in America while the act was in effect, but some did—and most of those who entered the country did so illegally. Therefore, the act may have served its purpose by severely limiting Chinese immigration, but it created a new problem for American society: illegal immigration.

The Chinese who did find a way to slip into America made use of what would become a familiar path for illegal immigrants.

Chinese laborers (pictured in California in 1877) built the nation's railroads with little more than picks, shovels, and wheelbarrows. Animosity toward Chinese immigrants peaked in 1882, when Congress passed a law banning most immigration from China.

First they found their way into Mexico; then they gained entry into the United States through remote border crossings—much as Mexicans and people from other Latin American states cross the border today. In fact, the US Bureau of Immigration (as it was known then) established the first border patrol in 1904. Border agents were mostly charged with picking up illegal Chinese immigrants making the trek across the deserts of the Southwest. As fewer Chinese people were available to perform the most menial and lowest-paying jobs, employers started looking toward other immigrants to fill these positions. They found willing workers in Mexican immigrants.

Revolution in Mexico

Many of the Mexican immigrants who took the undesirable jobs were anxious to leave their country. In addition to severe poverty, often caused by drought conditions, Mexicans had endured political turmoil that erupted in revolution in 1910. Over the course of the Mexican Revolution, some 600,000 Mexicans fled their country, most choosing to resettle to America.

Revolutionary activity dragged on for some 10 years. Then, in 1917, American intelligence agents intercepted a telegram in which German diplomats promised to return American territory to Mexico if Mexico would attack the US, thereby keeping the American army busy and out of Europe for the duration of World War I. None of these developments enhanced relations between Americans and immigrant Mexicans.

Congress responded by passing the Immigration Act of 1917, which barred criminals, mentally ill people, alcoholics, and others from immigrating to America. The act also barred illiterate people over the age of 16 from entering the country—a prohibition aimed directly at keeping poor Mexicans, who often had little or no schooling, from crossing the border legally. The act widened restrictions on Asian immigration, extending the earlier ban on Chinese immigration to include virtually all Asians. Another law, the Immigration Act of 1924, set quotas on the number of immigrants who could enter the country—this law was aimed mostly at the wave

"Our ancestors possessed a right, which nature has given to all men, of departing from the country in which chance, not choice, has placed them, of going in quest of new habitations, and of there establishing new societies."[13]

— Thomas Jefferson, third president of the United States.

of Europeans immigrating after World War I, but it applied to Mexicans as well.

The Guest Workers

The laws passed by Congress in the early twentieth century were effective in keeping immigrants out of the country, but soon a dire labor shortage would change attitudes toward immigration. During World War II most able-bodied American men were summoned to military service, creating a vast labor shortage. Congress responded by establishing the bracero program, permitting Mexican laborers—guest workers—to enter the country to work on American farms. (In English, bracero means "day laborer.") Following the war, influential American growers convinced the US government to keep the bracero program intact because the higher wages demanded by American workers would cut into their profits. US officials agreed, and braceros were allowed to continue to work on American farms. Indeed, in 1945—the year the war ended—50,000 braceros were working on American farms; in 1956 nearly a half-million braceros were picking crops in America.

However, even a half-million braceros could not keep up with the demand for cheap labor on farms in the Southwest. As a result, tens of thousands of illegal immigrants streamed across the border in search of farm labor jobs. In 1950 a presidential commission predicted dire consequences for American workers if the flow of illegal immigration was not better controlled. The commission found that most growers and other employers paid illegal immigrants wages that were half what they would have had to pay American workers. By 1954, it was estimated that some 4 million Mexicans were living in the United States illegally.

Operation Wetback

President Dwight D. Eisenhower decided that a crackdown was needed, and in 1954 a policy initiative known as Operation Wetback was set in motion to round up illegal immigrants and return them to Mexico. ("Wetback" is a derogatory term derived from the observation that many Mexicans crossed illegally into the United

Migrant workers from Mexico pick strawberries in California under the bracero program. By 1956, nearly 500,000 braceros were picking crops in the United States.

States by wading or swimming the Rio Grande River.) The program was modestly successful: in California, Texas, and Arizona, where Operation Wetback was concentrated, agents of the US Immigration and Naturalization Service rounded up some 130,000 illegal immigrants while another 1 million left voluntarily, fearing arrest. That put a dent in the illegal immigrant population in America but, certainly, the sweep did not stop people from crossing the border illegally. Moreover, under Operation Wetback, federal agents

typically put immigrants on buses, driving them across the border, to be discharged on Mexican soil. It is believed many simply waited until dark, then crossed back illegally.

By the 1960s, the civil rights movement that had swept through American society began to have an effect on immigration policy. Congress passed the Immigration and Nationality Act of 1965, which eliminated many of the limitations on immigration that had been adopted by the prior acts of 1917 and 1924. Quotas remained for each country of origin, but they were greatly expanded, and the emphasis for granting permission for entry was placed not on country of origin but on the reason for entering the country. Among those given preference for entry were people wishing to join their spouses. Also given preference were siblings and children of resident aliens or naturalized citizens, as well as students, professionals, scientists, and artists.

Amnesties for Illegal Immigrants

The 1965 act was well intentioned, but it had little effect on stemming the tide of illegal immigration, particularly since the bracero program had been discontinued the preceding year. In addition, growers and other employers still wanted cheap labor, and Mexicans and other Hispanics were more than willing to cross the border illegally to take the jobs. Indeed, many employers of illegal immigrant labor were not farms or sweatshop factories but wealthy Americans who sought housekeepers, cooks, gardeners, and nannies. As a result, thousands of illegal immigrants continued to stream in. Congress attempted to address this issue in 1986 with adoption of the Immigration Reform and Control Act, which made it a crime for American employers to knowingly hire illegal immigrants.

Four years later Congress adopted another measure. The Immigration Act of 1990 still maintained a quota system but greatly expanded the number of immigrants permitted to enter the country—under the old law, the limit had been set at 270,000 per year; the new law raised the number to 700,000. Meanwhile, a handful of amnesties were approved in the 1980s and 1990s, providing legal status for thousands of illegal immigrants who

NAFTA and Illegal Immigration

An international agreement that came into force in 1994, the North American Free Trade Agreement (NAFTA) eliminated tariffs on certain goods imported to the United States from Mexico and Canada, reducing the price of US products. Critics contended that NAFTA would cost jobs for Americans, because it would encourage many American companies to open manufacturing plants in Mexico, where labor costs are far lower than in the United States.

But if American companies are creating more jobs for Mexicans, wouldn't more Mexicans opt to stay in their home country rather than cross the border illegally, looking for work in the United States? That was the assumption, but it proved to be faulty.

For starters, although many American companies opened factories in Mexico, thereby creating jobs in that country, wages for Mexicans did not rise. Many workers at US-owned plants barely earn enough to sustain their families in Mexico and believe they would be far better off looking for work in the States. "The main thing that would have stemmed the flow of people across the border was a rapid increase in wages in Mexico," says Dani Rodrik, a Harvard University economist.

US officials also believe that while America has honored its agreement with Mexico by creating jobs, Mexican politicians have failed to keep up their end by improving roads, housing, and social services for Mexicans. Says economist Gary Hufbauer, "In a lot of [Mexican] cities the infrastructure is terrible, not even enough running water or electricity in poor neighborhoods. People get temporary jobs, but that is all."

Quoted in Louis Uchitelle, "NAFTA Should Have Stopped Illegal Immigration, Right?," *New York Times*, February 18, 2007. www.nytimes.com.

could prove they held jobs or were enrolled in college. Still, by the 1990s, it was clear that a new get-tough attitude was taking hold in Washington. President Bill Clinton enlarged and bolstered the US Border Patrol Service while, along the border, electronic sensors were installed to help law enforcement officers detect crossings. In addition, portions of the border were now being fenced. These measures continued under presidents George W. Bush and Barack Obama.

Illegal Immigration Declines

The firmer measures to control immigration have shown some results. According to a study by the Pew Hispanic Center, there were 11.1 million illegal immigrants living in America in 2009—a decline from 2007, when estimates of the number of illegal immigrants living in the country ran as high as 12 million. Sixty percent of those immigrants are from Mexico, but other Latin American countries, including Honduras, Guatemala, and El Salvador, account for 20 percent of the total; others make their way to America from Asian countries, mostly China and South Korea (11 percent); Europe and Canada (4 percent); and other countries (5 percent).

Moreover, the average influx declined as well. Between 2000 and 2005 approximately 850,000 illegal immigrants entered each year, but in 2009 the Pew Hispanic Center reported that number had declined to about 300,000 a year. Meanwhile, the federal government has stepped up deportations: according to US Immigration and Customs Enforcement, nearly 400,000 illegal immigrants were deported from October 2009 to September 2010—a record number.

Despite these results, there is no question that more than a century after President Arthur signed the first law restricting immigration, thus creating the problem of illegal immigration in America, many major laws and other policy changes have been implemented to address the issue and most have largely failed. Although experts, politicians, and others continue to debate whether illegal immigrants commit a disproportionate number of crimes, tax the American social network, and take jobs from Americans, the fact remains that more than 11 million foreign-born people are living in America illegally.

Facts

- From 1994 to 2007, during a period in which the illegal immigration population of America doubled, violent crime in America dropped by 34 percent, according to a study by the American Immigration Council of Washington, DC.

- A 2010 Pew Hispanic Center study concluded that a 22 percent drop in the illegal immigration rate between 2007 and 2009 had no impact on the availability of jobs for Americans.

- Overall, illegal immigrants make up about 4 percent of the US population, according to statistics provided by the Pew Hispanic Center and US Census Bureau.

- In 1996, the first year in which border fences were installed near San Diego, California; Nogales, Arizona; and El Paso and Brownsville, Texas, crime in those communities dropped by up to 30 percent.

- Immigration experts told the *Christian Science Monitor* in 2010 that 85 percent of Mexicans living in America have entered the country illegally.

- In the years before adoption of the Chinese Exclusion Act in 1882, an estimated 98 percent of immigrants who arrived at American borders were granted permission to enter the country.

Can America Effectively Seal Its Borders?

A tall steel fence stands between the communities of San Luis, Mexico, and San Luis, Arizona. Before the fence was erected, the area was a busy crossing point for illegal immigrants. But in 2006 security along portions of the US-Mexico border, including the San Luis area, was bolstered by the new barrier. By 2010, as a result of the fence, illegal immigration in the San Luis area had slowed to a trickle.

US Border Patrol officer Chad Smith regularly patrols the San Luis area in a helicopter. Years ago, Smith says, it was not uncommon for a single helicopter patrol to spot dozens of people crossing the border illegally. Now, he reports, helicopter crews patrolling the San Luis area usually spot only a handful of would-be immigrants trying to scale the formidable fence. Adds Border Patrol officer Mike Lowrie, "This used to be a very high-trafficked area, and now it is not."[14]

To people on both sides of the immigration debate, the border fence is more than simply a tall steel object that hinders illegal immigration: it is a symbol of the controversy. To those who favor taking the most dramatic measures to stem illegal immigration, the fence is an impenetrable wall that should be extended across the entire border. "The fence works," insists former US representative Duncan Hunter Sr. of California, a longtime advocate for staunching the flow of illegal immigrants. "Let's replicate this fence across the southwest border so we know who is coming into the country and what they're bringing with them."[15]

But to those who believe there are better ways to address illegal immigration, the border fence represents little more than a cruel and ineffective barrier that does not reflect America's long tradition of accepting the oppressed people of other nations. Says former US senator Mel Martinez, who immigrated to America from Cuba,

> I believe that America has always expressed the hopes and aspirations of the world. I believe that the symbol of America has always, to me, been the Statue of Liberty, a symbol of hope, opportunity, of welcoming and all that America symbolizes. . . . Immigrants don't come to America to change America. Immigrants come to America to be changed by America. And I believe that, if we give the opportunity to those new Americans that are now here illegally but which hope for a better life that we will then be building a better America.[16]

Sister Communities

For decades, "sister communities" like San Luis, Mexico, and San Luis, Arizona, treasured their close-knit relationships. It was not unusual for members of the same family to live on both sides of the border and to cross over regularly for visits. Of course people were expected to cross back at the end of the day, and most abided by the law.

A typical example of this relationship could be found just south of San Diego, California, along the state's border with Mexico, where Border Field State Park was established in 1974. People from Mexico and America were invited to use the park, which is adjacent to the Pacific Ocean, and mingle as friends and neighbors. A plaque mounted on a rock in the park says the facility was established to "symbolize the friendship between the peoples of the United States and Mexico."

Eventually, though, the Mexican and American sides of the park were divided by a fence. A US Border Patrol officer, quoted in the *Christian Science Monitor* newspaper, comments: "This used to be a nice place where people from here and over there could actually get together. Then all the illegal aliens and the drug runners ruined it."[17]

Fencing had been erected in various places along the border for many years, but in 1996 President Bill Clinton authorized the first program to bring the fencing under a coordinated federal policy. That year, 40 miles (65km) of chain-link fence went up in Texas, Arizona, and California where illegal border crossings were common. These first few miles of fencing were largely ineffective. Just 14 feet (4.3m) high, the fence did little to deter illegal immigrants. Moreover, many found it easy enough to simply hike around the fence or find places where others had cut through the chain-link mesh. "Anyone can plainly see this fence won't stop a flea," complains Arizona farmer Dawn Garner. "This [fence] is just too easy to cut into, climb over, and go under or around."[18]

Formidable Barrier

In 2006 Congress took steps to bolster the barrier, authorizing a $2.4-billion project to erect fencing along nearly 700 miles (1,125km) of the US-Mexico border. The plan was that as people with the intent to enter the United States illegally approached the border, they would not find a simple chain-link fence. Rather, under the plan approved by Congress, illegal crossers would face a formidable barrier separating them from American soil.

Duncan Hunter Sr., who formerly represented the San Diego area in the House of Representatives, was one of the driving forces behind winning funding for the fence. Shortly after Congress allocated the money for the fence, he said, "It's time we get serious about border control, do what's right, and build the border fence. Secure borders make America safer. What's so hard to understand about that?"[19] In fact, Hunter has called for the entire 1,950-mile border (3,140km) with Mexico to be fenced, but Congress provided the funds for just about a third of the border, instructing the federal Department of Homeland Security to select the most problematic areas of the border as sites for the barrier.

Depending on location, the border fence can feature as many as three tiers: a short "pedestrian fence" that is intended to keep people away from the main fence, a steel barricade as high as 21 feet (6.4m) that serves as the main deterrent to crossing, and a final chain-link fence that is capped with barbed wire. That is the typical configuration in urban areas, such as the San Luis region.

> "Anyone can plainly see this fence won't stop a flea. [It's] just too easy to cut into, climb over, and go under or around."[18]
>
> — Arizona farmer Dawn Garner.

Outside of cities, the pedestrian fence is often replaced by a barrier designed to impede vehicular traffic. "You can see the triple-layer fencing," Chad Smith, the Border Patrol officer, told a reporter as he flew over the San Luis portion of the fence. "I've known guys who have gone on a flight and come back [after observing] 100-plus illegals. . . . Now it's in single digits, typically."[20]

The Coyotes

The fence may be effective in the San Luis area and other places where the barrier has been erected; but since only about a third of the border has been fenced, there remains more than 1,000 miles (1,600km) of open country, where people who would not otherwise be admitted to the United States can freely cross into the country. Many of the immigrants enlist the aid of guides, known as "coyotes," to shepherd them across the remote areas of the border. Coyotes are familiar figures in Mexican border towns: many station themselves on busy street corners to greet those who straggle off buses, having been apprehended and deported by US immigration officials. One coyote, Tomas Romero, works out of Naco, Mexico, which is directly across the border from the town of Naco, Arizona. "Don't be depressed," he tells the deportees as they step off the bus. "There is a better place to cross!"[21]

The coyote business is lucrative. Most illegal immigrants pay $2,000 or more to be smuggled into the United States. Since the immigrants typically come from impoverished backgrounds, most have to sell all their possessions or go heavily into debt to raise the money for the coyote's fee.

In many cases, coyotes will load a group of paying customers into the back of a truck and drive them into the desert, finding places to cross far away from the border fence. As the patrols on the American side have become more vigilant, though, the coyotes have found it necessary to drive deeper into the desert. At some point, the road ends and the truck can go no further, which means that the final leg of the journey must be on foot. "I will tell them they will walk some but not much—maybe six hours,"[22] Romero says.

Actually, it is not unusual for illegal immigrants to spend several days in the desert. By the time they realize that Romero or another coyote has lied to them, it is too late to turn back. All they can do is endure the heat and the thirst as they hike across the searing scrubland.

The Border Fence and the Environment

Supporters of the border fence have come under fire from environmentalists, who believe the 700-mile barrier (1,125km) has harmed animal life along the US-Mexico border. Critics point to a portion of the barrier that has been erected through the Buenos Aires National Wildlife Refuge in Arizona, where the steel fence has been built through the habitats of jaguars, pygmy owls, and other species native to the region. "This is another example of the federal government riding roughshod over America's treasured lands and legal process in its rush to complete a highly ineffective and controversial border wall," says Matt Clark, the Southwest representative for the advocacy group Defenders of Wildlife.

Officials of the US Homeland Security Department contend, though, that they have taken measures to help protect wildlife. For example, in some portions of the fence tiny holes have been drilled into the wall to enable lizards and other small animals to pass through.

Former US representative Tom Tancredo, an advocate for the fence, believes the environmental impact of the barrier is minimal and that the real culprits are the illegal immigrants who leave trash behind as they cross. He says, "The environmental activists who scream about the possible impact of the fence are hypocritically silent about the degradation caused by the hundreds of pathways and tons of trash left behind by more than one million border invaders annually."

Quoted in Randal C. Archibold, "Border Fence Work Raises Environmental Concerns," *New York Times*, November 21, 2007. www.nytimes.com.

Tom Tancredo, "No Fence, No Border? No Bull," *Human Events*, May 28, 2008. www.human events.com.

Similar to Prohibition

The success that coyotes like Romero enjoy has prompted critics to question whether the erection of a border fence is truly a wise solution to the illegal immigration problem. A 2008 study by the University of California–San Diego found that despite the fence, more than half the illegal immigrants who attempt border crossings are successful on the first try. Many who are caught once simply try again; the study found that between 92 and 96 percent of illegal immigrants manage to eventually cross the border undetected. Indeed, the study determined that the most successful crossers are those who have hired coyotes.

Antonio Gonzalez, president of the San Antonio, Texas–based William C. Velasquez Institute, which studies economic and political issues involving Hispanic Americans, likens the border fence to the steps taken in the 1920s and 1930s to keep alcoholic beverages from entering the country. During the era of Prohibition, the federal government established a police force of agents to apprehend rumrunners and other smugglers from bringing liquor across the Canadian and Mexican borders. Those efforts were largely unsuccessful, and in 1933, after 13 years of futilely trying to stem the flow of alcohol, Prohibition was repealed by means of the Twenty-First Amendment. During the era of Prohibition, vast criminal enterprises headed by such mobsters as Al Capone grew around the liquor trade. Once Prohibition was repealed, Gonzalez says, the bottom fell out of the illegal liquor trade and criminals like Capone were put out of business. Gonzalez predicts that if America adopts a more receptive attitude toward illegal immigrants, the coyotes would be put out of business and there would be no need for a border fence. "The border fence is unworkable and ineffective," says Gonzalez. "We should learn from our history of alcohol prohibition . . . which spawned the 'booze mafias' [of] Al Capone. Repeal of alcohol prohibition in 1933 substantially reduced the endemic violent gangsterism of the time."[23]

> "It's time we get serious about border control, do what's right, and build the border fence. Secure borders make America safer. What's so hard to understand about that?"[19]
>
> — Former US representative Duncan Hunter Sr. of California.

People Who Overstay Their Visas

Critics of the border fence also argue that even if the barrier is extended across the entire US-Mexico border, it would not be effective in stemming the flow of people who enter the country legally but then overstay their visas. According to the US Department of Homeland Security, as many as 300,000 people a year overstay their visas, thus moving from the status of legal visitor to that of

illegal immigrant. "We are spending a lot of money and resources on protecting the border from those crossing illegally, but that's not the only way people are crossing the border,"[24] says Evelyn Cruz, a professor of immigration law at Arizona State University.

People who overstay their visas do not fit the stereotype of the border crosser—the impoverished Mexican or Salvadoran willing to risk his or her life in a hazardous trek across the desert. Rather, adult visa holders have already provided evidence to immigration officials that they have a legitimate purpose to enter the country and that they possess a degree of higher education, have a job, or are otherwise economically stable. Still, they have decided to overstay their visas because they find themselves in a better position to prosper in the United States than in their home countries.

Other opponents of the fence suggest the structure is simply not reflective of the American values proclaimed in the base of the Statue of Liberty. In 1903, words from the poem "The New Colossus" by Emma Lazarus were etched into the statue's base as

A coyote, or smuggler, drives hopeful migrants to a drop-off point in the Mexican desert. From there they will make the treacherous trek through the desert in hopes of crossing into the United States at the Arizona border.

a message of welcome to immigrants. The poem reads, "Give me your tired, your poor. Your huddled masses yearning to breathe free. Send these, the homeless, tempest-tost to me, I lift my lamp beside the golden door." Says Chris Liska Carger, an author and professor of bilingual education at Northern Illinois University, "Perhaps we should encircle Lady Liberty with a big fence and keep those undocumented, albeit 'hard-working' 'illegal aliens' away from there too. Her lamp beside the golden door wasn't meant to shine on them."[25]

Left to Die

As illegal immigrants venture further into the desert, they are putting their lives at risk. Many are victimized by the marauding *bajadores*. Others succumb to the harsh desert environment, dying of thirst or falling victim to sunstroke or heat exhaustion. According to an estimate published by the American Civil Liberties Union, more than 5,000 illegal immigrants have died in remote desert areas. "It's ridiculous that anybody has to die on that border," responds Raquel Rubio-Goldsmith, coordinator of the Binational Migration Institute of the University of Arizona. "We have to find some rational way to go about this."[26]

In 2007—the first year of the border fence—more than 200 bodies were found in remote portions of Pima County, Arizona. This represented a record number of immigrant deaths recorded in the county. As the fence has grown longer and border patrols more intensive, the deaths have continued. In 2010 more than 250 bodies, presumed to be those of illegal immigrants, were found in Pima County.

According to US immigration officials, most of the victims are elderly crossers who become ill and are left to die by the coyotes. Says Rev. John Herman, a Roman Catholic priest in San Luis, Arizona, "We know that the way enforcement has gone has driven many people into the desert and caused more deaths. Needless deaths."[27]

$18 Million per Mile

Arguments against the fence advanced by Gonzalez, Rubio-Goldsmith, and other critics have gained little traction among fence supporters who feel that the barrier has been effective. For-

Saving Lives in the Desert

Many illegal immigrants have been happy to find supplies of water in the desert. Tanks containing water have been stationed in strategic locations by Humane Borders, an organization of clergy members who hope to reduce the death toll in the desert. Says Rev. Robin Hoover, "We want to take death out of the equation."

Humane Borders came to be after the founders learned that a group of Arizona ranchers had been shooting at illegal immigrants. Several border crossers were killed, and later travelers decided to venture further into the desert to avoid the gunfire. This detour made the journey to the border longer, which resulted in more deaths from dehydration, since many of the crossers did not have enough water to survive the longer trip. To save lives, members of the clergy in Arizona border cities resolved to make water available to the crossers.

Humane Borders found an ally in the US Border Patrol, which recommended several sites for the water tanks. David Aguilar, a Border Patrol officer in Tucson, Arizona, says his agency does not want to see people die in the desert, either. However, Aguilar said, the Border Patrol keeps a close watch over Humane Borders because some of its members are suspected of harboring illegal immigrants in their churches. Says Aguilar, "There is a line they must not cross."

Quoted in Elaine Rivera, "Mercy Mission in the Desert," *Time*, June 11, 2001, p. 56.

mer US representative Tom Tancredo of Colorado, an advocate for the fence during his years in Congress, points out that federal immigration authorities have long made temporary visas available to Mexican citizens who wish to cross over for brief periods, usually to visit family members or conduct business.

These visas permit Mexicans to remain on the American side of the border for up to 72 hours. Some 6 million Mexican citizens have obtained the visas, he says, and most return without over-staying the 72-hour period. "Any Mexican citizen with legitimate business in [America] has no difficulty crossing the border through a port of entry," says Tancredo. "The only travelers who will be inconvenienced by the border fence are people trying to enter our country illegally or smuggle drugs or other contraband."[28]

While the effectiveness of the border fence is debated, another method employed by the US government to close the border has been regarded as a failure. At the time the border fence was conceived in 2006, proponents for closing the border also proposed high-tech methods for monitoring activity by illegal crossers. Congress approved construction of a "virtual fence" that would include a network of high-tech sensors, cameras, and radar monitoring equipment designed to detect movement along the border.

In 2011 the Department of Homeland Security killed the project, citing cost overruns and questions about whether the system is effective. The project, which was planned to provide surveillance for the entire 1,950-mile border (3,140-km) was projected to cost $8 billion by 2017. Instead, the virtual fence has already cost more than $1 billion and, by 2011, was providing security for just 53 miles (85km). The decision was reached after the investigation arm of Congress, the Government Accountability Office, found that the sensors can't tell the difference between humans and between animals or humans and vehicles. The cost of some $18 million per mile led the GAO to question the value of the virtual fence. According to Cameron County, Texas, judge Carlos Cascos, "It has been an utter failure."[29]

Bolstering the Border Patrol

In addition to trying to monitor activity by illegal immigrants through high-tech methods, the federal government has invested heavily in putting more boots on the ground. In 1992 the US Border Patrol consisted of some 3,500 officers; by 2010 there were more than 20,000 officers.

Moreover, a $600 million package approved by Congress in 2010 added 1,000 officers to the Border Patrol, 250 officers to US Customs and Border Protection, and 250 officers to US Immigra-

"We know that the way enforcement has gone has driven many people into the desert and caused more deaths. Needless deaths."[27]

— Rev. John Herman, priest in San Luis, Arizona.

tion and Customs Enforcement. The package of aid also included funds to buy new equipment, including drone aircraft to monitor border crossings from above.

Meanwhile, the Defense Department has deployed National Guard troops to the border states to help bolster efforts by the Border Patrol. From 2006 to 2008, some 6,000 National Guard troops patrolled the border. The policy was implemented again in August 2010, when 1,200 National Guard troops were deployed to the border regions in Arizona, Texas, California, and New Mexico. The initiative drew this response from Arizona attorney general Terry Goddard: "It will help. Manpower clearly has been deficient."[30]

Police empty barrels of beer into a sewer during Prohibition. Prohibition-era laws failed to halt the manufacture and sale of alcohol in the United States. Some experts warn that the border fence will have much the same effect on illegal immigration.

Crossing the Canadian Border

Immigration officers don't just patrol deserts in the American Southwest. They look for illegal crossers in border cities and sometimes in places far from the borders. In the months following the terrorist attacks of 2001, Congress provided the Department of Homeland Security with the authority to demand identification from suspicious persons within 100 miles (160km) of all American borders.

The power was intended as a tool to fight terrorism, but since 2008 the department has been using the authority to apprehend illegal immigrants in areas far from national borders. Many times, those searches are conducted aboard trains.

Agents board trains that approach within 100 miles of the borders and demand passports or other identification papers from passengers. This policy is not confined to the border with Mexico—many passengers have been questioned near the Canadian border as well. "It's turned into a police state on the northern border," says Cary M. Jensen, director of international services for the University of Rochester in New York, which is attended by many foreign citizens who study there on student visas. "It's essentially become an internal document check."[31]

Internal Passports

To help immigration officers identify illegal immigrants, some political leaders have called for the issuance of national identity cards. The cards would be issued to every citizen, with the data on the cards entered into a national computer database. Therefore, immigration officials could inspect a card and, through an instant computer check, learn the status of the cardholder, even determining whether the card is fraudulent, indicating that the person carrying it is in the country illegally.

Legislation to establish the card system was proposed in 2010 by two US senators, Charles Schumer of New York and Lindsey Graham of South Carolina. The senators compared the documents to the cards issued to all Americans by the Social Security Administration. These cards contain the citizen's Social Security number, which is required to obtain a job, file income tax returns, and qualify for various benefits provided by the federal government. In a statement, the senators said, "We would require all U.S. citizens and legal immigrants who want jobs to obtain a high-tech, fraud-proof . . . card."[32]

Civil libertarians have long considered abhorrent the notion of instituting a national identity card system, regarding it as a step toward creation of a totalitarian state. Says the American Civil Liberties Union:

"Any Mexican citizen with legitimate business in [America] has no difficulty crossing the border through a port of entry. The only travelers who will be inconvenienced by the border fence are people trying to enter our country illegally."[28]

— Tom Tancredo, former member of the US House of Representatives.

Americans have long had a visceral aversion to building a society in which the authorities could act like totalitarian sentries and demand "your papers please!" And that everyday intrusiveness would be conjoined with the full power of modern computer and database technology. When a police officer or security guard scans your ID card with his pocket bar-code reader, for example, will a permanent record be created of that check, including the time and your location? How long before office buildings, doctors' offices, gas stations, highway tolls, subways and buses incorporate the ID card into their security or payment systems for greater efficiency? The end result could be a nation where citizens' movements inside their own country are monitored and recorded through these "internal passports."[33]

Can Illegal Immigrants Be Kept Out?

As illegal immigrants continue to cross the border between the United States and Mexico, much of the debate centers on the 700-mile fence (1,125km) as well as the other measures taken by the federal government to police the border and keep people from crossing illegally. Many critics believe that the 1,950-mile border (3,140km) with Mexico cannot be adequately monitored even with the best electronic surveillance equipment and more than 20,000 Border Patrol officers—that there are too many remote areas in which undocumented persons can slip illegally into America. "The nation is caught between the forces saying something must be done and the practicalities that it can't properly be executed," says Patricia Hamm, assistant professor of political science at Iowa State University. "And so we end up with what we've got—so many miles of wall that officials can point to from Washington to say 'We've done it.' And local residents and others who see what's in front of them and say, 'It doesn't matter, it won't work.'"[34]

Others disagree, contending that the fence and the increased personnel made available by the Border Patrol and National Guard have been effective. "The border is more secure and more resourced than it has ever been, but there is more to be done,"[35] insists Alan Bersin, commissioner of US Customs and Border Protection. Clearly, though, neither side is happy with the results. Supporters of the fence and the other get-tough policies believe too many illegal immigrants are still finding ways to cross the border. Meanwhile, some critics believe there is really no effective means of keeping them out while others do not think that American lawmakers have the right to bar desperate people in need.

Facts

- A 2010 poll by the public opinion research agency Rasmussen Reports found that 68 percent of Americans favor continuing construction of the border fence.

- Prior to construction of the border fence, the typical fee charged by a coyote to smuggle an immigrant into America was $800; now that the fence has made it tougher to cross, coyotes have more than doubled their fees.

- In 2007, the first full year following erection of the border fence, the US Homeland Security Department said that apprehensions of illegal immigrants along the Mexican border had dropped by 20 percent.

- By 2011 the federal government had no plans to extend the 700-mile border fence (1,125km); maintaining the existing barrier, however, is expected to cost $6.5 billion through 2030.

- The US Border Patrol office in Rochester, New York, arrested 1,040 illegal border crossers in 2008—most were taken into custody on buses and trains traveling near the Canadian border.

- The term "coyote" may have originated in 1923 when a Texas newspaper reported the murders of six Italian immigrants who paid Mexican guides to lead them across the US border. A police official alleged that the guides had killed the immigrants, derisively calling the murderers "coyotes" and "wolves of the border."

Can Illegal Immigration Be Policed Within US Borders?

L
ocated some 2,000 miles (3,220km) from the Mexican border, the coal-mining town of Hazleton, Pennsylvania, would appear to be an unlikely place to find concern about illegal immigration. But that is not the case. The Hispanic share of the population of Hazleton has grown from about 5 percent in 2000 to more than 30 percent in 2010. Officials in Hazleton suspect that a large percentage of the Hispanic residents of their town are living in America illegally. "When you start seeing serious crimes being committed, very violent crimes being committed and time and time again those involved are illegal aliens, it doesn't take a brain surgeon to figure out that you're experiencing a problem here that you've never had before, nor do you have the resources to deal with it,"[36] says Lou Barletta, a former mayor of Hazleton.

Barletta and other Hazleton officials believed they had found the answer to their problem when they adopted an ordinance in 2006 that gave the city the power to suspend business licenses to Hazleton companies found to be employing illegal aliens. The ordinance also gave the city the power to withdraw landlord licenses from building owners identified as renting homes or apartments to illegal immigrants.

The effort by Hazleton officials was born of frustration. In Hazleton and other cities and towns, as well as in many states, political leaders saw the effects of illegal immigration on local communities. Unwilling to wait for the federal government to act, state and local officials have taken matters into their own hands. They have resorted to crafting local ordinances and laws they hope will bar illegal immigrants as effectively as any fence made of steel or concrete. Says Gregory Minchak, a spokesperson for the National League of Cities, "Because of the absence of the feds doing anything, there's a lot of financial, cultural, political strains that are occurring [in cities and states]. They are just starting to act on their own."[37]

Mired in Litigation

Although the ordinance in Hazleton was intended to punish business owners and landlords, another purpose was clear: to encourage illegal immigrants to leave town. City officials believed that if enough pressure could be placed on people who employ illegal immigrants or provide them with homes, Hazleton would become a less hospitable place, and illegal immigrants would go elsewhere. "We're not involved in immigration in any way," insists Barletta. "We're not regulating people coming in and out of the country. In fact, we're not doing anything to the illegal alien. We're simply punishing businesses that hire them and landlords who rent to them."[38]

After Hazleton adopted its ordinance, several other communities adopted similar measures. Among them was Fremont, Nebraska, which in 2010 adopted an ordinance that also penalized employers and landlords who provide jobs and homes to illegal immigrants. According to a study by the University of Nebraska, fewer than 200 Hispanics lived in Fremont in 1990; by 2009, Hispanics made up nearly 10 percent of the Fremont population. Town officials suspect the increase in the Hispanic population is due to illegal immigrants finding homes in Fremont. In the Nebraska town and elsewhere, illegal immigrants seek the same opportunities for employment that are available in the border communities of Arizona, Texas, and California. "We all have to play by the same rules," insists lifelong Fremont resident Clint Walraven, who supports the measure. "If you want to stay here, get legal."[39]

The ordinances adopted in Fremont, Hazleton, and other communities have never gone into effect. Soon after their adoption, they were challenged in court by civil libertarians, Hispanic rights organizations, and similar groups. While the ordinances remain mired in litigation, the courts have barred their enforcement.

"When you start seeing serious crimes being committed, very violent crimes being committed and time and time again those involved are illegal aliens, it doesn't take a brain surgeon to figure out that you're experiencing a problem here that you've never had before."[36]

— Lou Barletta, former mayor of Hazleton, Pennsylvania.

Responsibility of the Federal Government

Leaders of the Hispanic community and others bristled at the ordinances in Hazleton and Fremont, suggesting they are racist measures that will ultimately harm Hispanic Americans as well as visitors who obtain green cards, which allow noncitizens to remain in the country legally. Critics suggested that in avoiding the possibility that they would hire or rent to illegal immigrants, business owners and landlords would refuse all requests for jobs or apartments from people of Hispanic ethnicity. Said Witold J. Walczak, legal director of the Pennsylvania chapter of the American Civil Liberties Union, which challenged the

Hazleton measure, "Hazleton pioneered a wave of these divisive laws across that country that tore communities apart along racial and ethnic lines."[40]

Hazleton's ordinance was tossed out by a federal judge in 2007. City officials appealed, but a federal appeals court upheld the ruling in 2010, finding that the ordinance was in fact ultimately aimed at regulating immigration. The court ruled that regulating immigration is a responsibility of the federal government—not local communities—and is specifically addressed in Article 1, Section 8, of the Constitution, which states that it is the responsibility of Congress "to establish a uniform rule of naturalization."

The courts may have ruled against the ordinance in Hazleton, but the voters in Hazleton as well as Fremont have made their feelings clear. In Fremont the illegal immigration control measure was approved in a referendum—meaning that all the citizens of Fremont had an opportunity to vote on the ordinance. In the Nebraska community, about 57 percent of the voters cast ballots to adopt the ordinance, with the remainder opposed.

Meanwhile, in Hazleton and nearby communities the voters used the 2010 election to express their feelings about illegal immigration. Running largely on a platform in which he pledged to crack down on illegal immigration, Barletta, the Hazleton mayor, was elected to Congress. Shortly after winning the seat, Barletta said he would turn his attention to controlling illegal immigration at the border, helping states such as Arizona contend with their porous borders with Mexico. He said, "Hopefully, my perspective will get the attention of others in Congress, and as a nation, we'll be able to do something about the problem of illegal immigration. We're seeing it escalate, especially in the state of Arizona and the southern states, where many of the problems in northern Mexico are spilling now."[41]

Arizona Cracks Down

Arizona is, in fact, at ground zero in the illegal immigration debate thanks to a state law adopted in 2010. The law is regarded as one of the toughest measures passed by a state or local government with the aim of policing illegal immigration. Provisions of the law include:

Few Legal Protections for Illegal Immigrants

The Constitution guarantees many rights to American citizens charged with crimes. Among these are the right to hear the charges against them in a public court of law, the right to a speedy trial, and the right to appeal. In contrast, illegal immigrants have few rights under American law.

For example, immigration agents do not need a warrant to enter the home of an illegal immigrant. That is, they do not require an order signed by a judge who believes that grounds exist to allow police to enter a given person's home. "Immigration law enforcement is all about getting you to where you belong, which is outside the United States," said Jan C. Ting, a law professor at Temple University in Philadelphia. "A lot of constitutional protections that one would normally expect in a criminal case do not necessarily apply."

In addition, under federal law, illegal immigrants can be taken into custody without being read *Miranda* warnings, which advise arrested persons of their rights, including the right to remain silent. Moreover, a person detained under suspicion of being an illegal immigrant can ask to speak to a lawyer, but the request will be granted only if he or she can pay the attorney's fee. Under law, the government has no responsibility to provide free legal counsel to an illegal immigrant.

Quoted in Julia Preston, "No Need for a Warrant, You're an Immigrant," *New York Times*, October 14, 2007. www.nytimes.com.

- Permission for police officers to use considerations of race and ethnicity, along with other factors, as reasons to question people whom they suspect of being in the country illegally.
- A requirement that local police officers investigate the immigration status of individuals if they suspect those individuals may be in the country illegally. Among the people whose

immigration status is to be checked are those whose vehicles are stopped by police for minor traffic violations.

- The mandatory detention of people who cannot immediately verify that they are in the country legally. In other words, somebody who receives a traffic citation can be arrested and held in jail if that person is unable to prove hat he or she is a citizen or the holder of a green card.
- Permission granted to police to make warrantless arrests of people they suspect of committing crimes that could lead to deportation. In other words, anybody suspected of a crime can be taken into custody and denied access to a lawyer while that person's immigration status is reviewed. If the person in custody is found to be a legal visitor or even a citizen, attorneys can assert that he or she had been denied certain basic rights under the Constitution.
- Criminal penalties imposed on employers who provide jobs to illegal immigrants.

The law was enacted in the weeks following the murder of Rob Krentz, the Arizona rancher who was killed in a remote desert area slightly north of the Mexican border. Hastily drafted and approved by the Arizona legislature, the bill was signed into law by Governor Jan Brewer on April 23, 2010—just 27 days after Krentz's body was found. "The fact that it got passed has a lot to do with the reflection and response to the Rob Krentz murder," says Cochise County, Arizona, sheriff Larry Dever, who investigated the Krentz case. "We cannot sit by while our citizens are terrorized, robbed and murdered by ruthless and desperate people who enter our country illegally."[42]

Fear of Racial Profiling

Critics of the Arizona measure fear the law will enable police to employ racial profiling—a widely illegal practice in which police use race or ethnicity as probable cause for suspecting that an individual has committed a crime. (Probable cause is the legal threshold police must establish for acting on the suspicion that a crime has been committed—hearing gunshots inside an apartment would be sufficient "probable cause" to allow a police officer who heard the shots to break down the door.) The practice of racial profiling surfaced as a controversial law enforcement technique in the 1990s as police agencies were able to develop statistical data identifying those who are likely to be drug dealers and similar criminals. In addition to race and ethnicity, such criminal profiles frequently focus on gender, age, and the types of car the drug dealers prefer.

Racial profiling has been denounced by many political leaders—23 state legislatures have specifically outlawed its use as a law enforcement tool. Moreover, several innocent people who have been stopped, searched, and detained by police on suspicion of drug trafficking have been able to prove in court that they were singled out solely because of their race or ethnicity. In many cases, plaintiffs have been awarded huge cash damages after a court determination that they had been racially profiled.

"*We cannot sit by while our citizens are terrorized, robbed and murdered by ruthless and desperate people who enter our country illegally.*"[42]

— Cochise County, Arizona, sheriff Larry Dever.

As Brewer signed the law in Arizona, many legal experts and leaders of the Hispanic American community and others predicted that the measure would give a free hand to police to identify persons as suspects based solely on their ethnicity. "In practice, it is inevitable that this law will lead to racial profiling," says David Cole, professor at Georgetown University Law School in Washington, DC "People don't wear signs saying that they are illegal immigrants, nor do illegal immigrants engage in any particular behavior that distinguishes them from legal immigrants and citizens. So police officers will not stop white people, and will stop Latinos, especially poor Latinos."[43]

Critics also took issue with other provisions of the law, particularly the measure that gives police the authority to demand identification papers from those they question about immigration status during routine traffic stops. In a country where national ID cards continue to be a unpopular idea, critics found the measure similar to conditions in totalitarian states. "It is absolutely reminiscent of second class status of Jews in Germany prior to World War II when they had to have their papers with them at all times and were subject to routine inspections at the suspicion of being Jewish," US representative Jared Polis of Colorado said after the Arizona law was passed. "I fear that Arizona is headed for a police state and it really underscores the need for immigration reform at the federal level to fix our system."[44]

Intolerable Situation

Supporters of the Arizona law insist that while the anti-immigrant measures may seem harsh, they are needed because the current situation is intolerable. Says David Frum, a conservative political commentator and former White House speechwriter,

> Imagine yourself a landowner in southern Arizona. The border between San Diego and Tijuana is now effectively fenced, so the flow of illegal immigration has been diverted to your front yard. Every morning you wake up to a hillock of garbage: plastic bottles, food remains, human urine and feces. If you try to police your land, you put your life at risk. . . .
>
> Mexico's drug war has reached into Arizona cities. Federal authorities capture an average of 1.5 tons of marijuana per day in Arizona. Drug-related kidnappings, tortures, and murders of illegals by illegals have made Phoenix one of the most violent cities in the United States. Illegals crowd hospital emergency rooms, crash uninsured cars, and transform overbuilt neighborhoods into rooming house slums.[45]

In defending the law, Arizona's governor and other state officials said they had grown frustrated with the federal government's failure to adopt immigration reform and believed that they had to implement their own laws—and that such measures were long overdue in Arizona, where illegal immigrants are estimated to compose nearly 6 percent of the state's population. It was a sentiment shared by officials in other states: shortly after Arizona passed its law, legislators in 24 other states said they were prepared to write similar measures.

Thousands of people march in Arizona to protest a 2010 state law aimed at identifying, prosecuting, and deporting illegal immigrants. Critics of the law say it will lead to harassment and discrimination against Hispanics regardless of their citizenship status.

Not a State Responsibility

By 2011, proposed state anti-immigration measures remained largely on hold because court challenges to the Arizona law meant that most of its provisions were not being enforced. For example, opponents of the Arizona law persuaded a federal judge to bar implementation of the parts of the law they believe to be unfair or unconstitutional. Among the provisions that were challenged were those that opponents fear could lead to racial profiling by police. Challenges to the legality of the Arizona law are expected to take several years to work their way through the courts.

Civil libertarians, Hispanic American groups, and other opponents found an ally in their cause in the federal government, which initiated a lawsuit against Arizona soon after Brewer signed the law. In filing the lawsuit, the Department of Justice contended that according to Article 1, Section 8, of the Constitution, enforcement of immigration law is solely the responsibility of the federal government and that state and local governments have no authority to assume such duties. It was the same argument opponents of the Hazleton ordinance had used in their successful challenge of that measure. Says US attorney general Eric Holder, "Setting immigration policy and enforcing immigration law is a national responsibility. A patchwork of state laws will only create more problems than it solves."[46]

Brewer reacted harshly to the federal government's opposition to the Arizona law, saying, "As a direct result of failed and inconsistent federal enforcement, Arizona is under violent attack from violent Mexican drug and immigrant smuggling cartels. Now, Arizona is under attack in federal court from President Obama and his Department of Justice."[47]

"I fear that Arizona is headed for a police state and it really underscores the need for immigration reform at the federal level to fix our system."[44]

— US representative Jared Polis of Colorado.

Proof of Legal Residency

With measures like those adopted in Arizona and Hazleton facing extensive legal challenges, some states are looking at their existing laws and changing them in ways less accommodating to illegal immigrants. Most of these efforts focus on driver's licenses, since these essential documents traditionally could be obtained without proof of citizenship, hence were readily available to illegal immigrants.

America's Toughest Sheriff

Long before the Arizona legislature adopted the controversial law aimed at reducing illegal immigration, Maricopa County, Arizona, sheriff Joe Arpaio—who calls himself "America's toughest sheriff"—ordered his deputies to conduct sweeps through neighborhoods where he suspects many illegal immigrants make their homes. Typically, Arpaio's deputies stop people for minor infractions—including jaywalking—then question them about their immigration status. The sweeps have resulted in the arrests of about 500 illegal immigrants a year.

Critics have charged Arpaio with racial profiling, but the sheriff has defended his methods. He says,

> When you have a legitimate contact during law enforcement operations, you should be able to ask for identification which law enforcement does anyway on a daily basis. You ask for ID and you see if that person is here illegally by checking out the immigration status of the person. We don't go around picking people off the streets because they look like they're from another country just because of their race.

Still, in 2009 the US Department of Justice launched an investigation of Arpaio on suspicion that the sheriff had violated the civil rights of Hispanic Americans. When federal investigators demanded the arrest records of the Maricopa County Sheriff's Office, Arpaio refused to turn them over. By 2011, the courts had not yet ordered Arpaio to turn over the records, but the sheriff said he had decided to temporarily suspend the sweeps.

Quoted in Nicholas Riccardi, "US Sues Arizona Sheriff in Rights Probe," *Philadelphia Inquirer*, September 3, 2010, p. A2.

Joe Arpaio, "Arizona Immigration Law," *Washington Post*, April 30, 2010. www.washingtonpost.com.

In 2011 Hawaii, Maine, New Mexico, Utah, and Washington State were maintaining very liberal policies that enabled undocumented immigrants to obtain driver's licenses. Officials in those states argue that illegal immigrants will drive anyway, and it is much safer for them to be tested to determine their qualifications to drive properly under the laws of their respective states.

But officials in other states have taken a new look at the issue and toughened their standards, requiring substantial proof of legal residency before they will issue the licenses. Among the states that have recently changed their standards are California, Michigan, Oregon, and Maryland. In Oregon officials acknowledged that they had made the requirements to obtain driver's licenses stricter out of fear that illegal immigrants would flock to the state to obtain a form of official identification—the license—that could be submitted to counter accusations that they are in the country illegally. "Oregon is one of the few states in the country that didn't have these ID requirements for driver's licenses," says Patty Wentz, a spokesperson for Governor Ted Kulongoski. "That made us one of the weak links."[48]

Workplace Raids

The basic charge by Arizona governor Brewer and other state officials—that the federal government has been ineffective in rooting out illegal immigrants—is often challenged by federal authorities. Indeed, there are several federal agencies that address immigration issues. Among them are US Customs and Border Protection, which includes the Border Patrol; US Immigration and Customs Enforcement, which is the chief investigatory agency for illegal immigration cases; and US Citizen and Immigration Services, which issues visas to legal immigrants and supervises their applications for citizenship. In 2010 Congress allocated nearly $20 billion to the three agencies.

In addition, other federal agencies address immigration issues. The Department of Justice provides state and local governments $330 million a year under the State Criminal Alien Assistance Program. These funds help state and local police investigate crimes and prosecute defendants found to be in the country illegally. Also funded by the federal government is the Secure Communities program, which conducts fingerprint checks on all people booked into US jails as a method of determining whether the detainees are in the country illegally. Each year, the Secure Communities program provides about $200 million to state and county jails.

Federal authorities are also known to conduct "workplace raids," in which immigration agents make unannounced visits to companies they suspect of employing undocumented workers. Critics contend, though, that the workplace raids do more harm than good. Typically, a male worker who lacks papers is arrested, taken into custody, and deported. Many times, the worker is a father who is supporting a family. When the father is deported, the mother and children are left behind with no financial support. Representative Luis Gutierrez, a member of Congress from Illinois, has called on the federal government to cease workplace raids. "You have single mothers now," Gutierrez says. "You have young, 15-year-old kids with no father. Think about that a moment."[49]

Still, federal authorities insist they are dedicated to policing the illegal immigration cases. Indeed, in 2008 more than 350,000 illegal immigrants were taken into custody and deported. That number has doubled since 1999.

"Setting immigration policy and enforcing immigration law is a national responsibility. A patchwork of state laws will only create more problems than it solves."[46]

— US attorney general Eric Holder.

For the Courts to Decide

Clearly, the measures in places like Arizona as well as Hazleton, Pennsylvania, and Fremont, Nebraska, face many legal hurdles before they can be implemented. The efforts behind those measures show the frustration of local officials whose constituents demand they take action against illegal immigration. The responses by those communities have provided legal tests that are likely to take years for the courts to sort out. Among these complicated issues are whether the federal government has sole authority over policing immigration and whether racial profiling can be used to identify illegal immigrants. It will be up to the courts to determine whether these measures pass constitutional muster or whether they are destined to join the long list of failed attempts to control illegal immigration.

Facts

- The first state that tried to enforce its own immigration law was Pennsylvania, which in 1939 adopted a measure requiring immigrants to carry identification cards; the US Supreme Court threw out the measure in 1941, finding it unconstitutional.

- Hazleton mayor Lou Barletta won election to Congress in 2010 by defeating an incumbent who had held the seat for 26 years; Barletta won with 54 percent of the vote.

- Nine states have adopted laws giving illegal immigrants who are students the right to pay discounted in-state tuition rates at state universities. Those states are California, New Mexico, Kansas, Nebraska, Illinois, New York, Texas, Utah, and Washington.

- A 2010 poll by the Gallup Organization found that 39 percent of Americans favor Arizona's tough law that allows active policing of illegal immigration, while 30 percent oppose the measure with the rest undecided. In Arizona, polling found 70 percent in favor of the measure.

- In 2008 nearly 6,300 illegal immigrants taken into custody by federal agents during workplace raids were deported.

- According to the Center for Immigration Studies, Arizona is home to one of the fastest-growing populations of illegal immigrants in the country: it increased from 330,000 in 2000 to 560,000 in 2008.

Can Other Countries Serve as Models for US Policies?

Each year, dozens of tiny boats attempt to cross the Mediterranean Sea. They embark from the northern coast of Africa, carrying men, women, and children who hope to escape the terrible poverty of many of Africa's cities and small villages for new opportunities in Europe. To book passage for the trip, the would-be immigrants seek out human traffickers, who find them seats on the boats. These traffickers are similar to the coyotes who guide illegal immigrants across the US-Mexico border.

Many of the boats aim for the southern coast of Spain. Some of the boats make it across, but others are not as fortunate. Some boats are intercepted by the Servicio Maritimo de la Guardia Civil—the Spanish coast guard—which detains the passengers and sends them back to Africa. Because the boats are often jerry-built and ramshackle, however, many would-be immigrants face a much worse fate. Poorly equipped to endure a voyage of several hundred miles across choppy waters, the tiny boats frequently capsize; fatalities among passengers are common.

In 2010 the Spanish coast guard intercepted a small boat carrying 40 illegal immigrants from Nigeria, Morocco, and Cameroon. The coast guard vessel guided the boat to the Spanish island of Alborán, about 40 miles (65km) south of the European main-land. When coast guard officers approached the craft, they were surprised to find a newborn baby. The child had been born to a Nigerian woman just as the boat landed on the Alborán beach. "The child's father . . . was carrying the baby in his arms, and it

Would-be immigrants, traveling in a crowded, rickety boat from Africa, reach an island under Spanish control. Many die trying to make the dangerous sea crossing; others are apprehended by Spanish authorities and deported.

still had 10 or 15 centimeters of umbilical cord hanging off,"[50] recalls coast guard officer Enrique Garberí. Medical personnel were called to the scene. The woman and her baby were taken to a hospital.

While the others aboard the boat were taken into custody and later deported, the woman and her baby did not have to go back to Africa. Under Spanish law, babies born in Spain, regardless of the nationalities of their parents, are entitled to remain in the country. The law also provides legal residency status for the mothers of the babies. The fortuitous timing of the baby's arrival—as the boat landed on the sandy Alborán beach—meant that the baby and her mother could stay in Spain.

Regularización in Spain

Illegal immigration is not unique to America. Across the globe, other countries have found their borders as porous as the border that separates Mexico from America. And, like America, they have struggled to secure their borders while attempting to fashion policies that would find ways to provide legal entry to some people who would be illegal immigrants if they made their way into their destinations now.

> "I feel bad because I know how hard it is for them to reach Spain, how they suffer and under what poor conditions some of them have to live."[52]
>
> — Jorge Ollero Perin, a government employee in the Spanish city of Huelva.

According to figures compiled by the United Nations, more than 200 million people are not citizens of the countries where they make their homes. This number represents growth of 60 percent over the past decade. As many as 20 percent of those immigrants—or up to 40 million people—may have entered their new countries illegally. If 11 million of them are living in America, then nearly 30 million illegal immigrants may have found homes elsewhere. "People are always on the move," says April Shipper, a global immigration expert at the University of California at Los Angeles. "People were moving before there were nations; people move in spite of nations. I don't think that will ever stop."[51]

Because it lies across the Mediterranean Sea from Africa, Spain pays close attention to its southern coastline. The Spanish coast guard constantly patrols the Mediterranean, seizing boatloads of illegal immigrants and sending them back to their home countries.

Spain's crackdown on illegal immigration represents a change in policy for the country, which until recently maintained an extremely friendly attitude toward immigrants—even illegal immigrants. By 2010, one in seven people living in Spain—or about 6.5 million people—had moved there from other countries. Many of them slipped into Spain illegally.

These illegal immigrants were, for the most part, permitted to stay. The Spanish name for the country's friendly policy toward immigration is *regularización*—or, in English, "regularization." As the name suggests, the government aimed to modify the status of certain illegal immigrants—in other words, to make them legal residents of Spain. Over the course of 25 years, Spanish lawmakers adopted six *regularizacións*, providing legal status to more than 1 million illegal immigrants.

Regularización is similar to the American amnesties of the 1980s and 1990s. With the Spanish economy booming, the country was in dire need of cheap labor to take jobs of the types most Spaniards were likely to reject—farm work and heavy manual labor, as well as housekeeping and child care. *Regularización* made Spain one of the most immigrant-friendly countries on earth. For years, many illegal immigrants streamed into the country, knowing Spanish law was lenient and that they would likely be permitted to stay.

Economy Sours

But in the latter half of the 2000 decade, the Spanish economy soured. In 2010 unemployment in Spain was as high as 20 percent, meaning that one in five Spaniards was out of work. As a result, many Spaniards became willing to take the low-paying, physically demanding jobs that would otherwise go to immigrant laborers.

Now many of the unemployed are immigrants, and many of those immigrants are in Spain illegally. As a result, Spanish authorities are cracking down—rounding up illegal immigrants and sending them home. "I feel bad because I know how hard it is for them to reach Spain, how they suffer and under what poor conditions

Plight of the Roma

French authorities have raided shantytowns, rounding up members of an ethnic group called the Roma—also known as gypsies—who have drifted into France from Romania. French officials insist that the shantytowns are plagued by squalor and disease. They accuse the Roma of exploiting their children by making them beg in the streets. Meanwhile, Roma women have been arrested on prostitution charges.

In several sweeps conducted in 2010, the arrested Roma have each been given 300 euros, or about $380, and put aboard airplanes bound for Bucharest, the Romanian capital. Although immigration officials in America, Europe, and elsewhere frequently conduct sweeps of neighborhoods where they suspect illegal immigrants have found shelter, French authorities have come under criticism for their campaign against the Roma because the Roma may not actually be illegal immigrants.

Romania and France are both members of the European Union, the 27-nation alliance of European countries. Under EU rules, citizens of member nations enjoy unfettered travel from country to country within the union. "We support unconditionally the right of every Romanian citizen to travel without restrictions within the EU," says Romanian president Traian Basescu. French officials insist they are acting within their country's law, which states that while EU citizens can travel freely in France, their stays are limited to three months unless they find employment.

Quoted in BBC News, "France Sends Roma Gypsies Back to Romania," August 20, 2010. www. bbc.co.uk.

some of them have to live,"[52] says Jorge Ollero Perin, a government employee who lives in the city of Huelva in southern Spain.

With no way to earn a living and chased out of their homes in cities, many of Spain's illegal immigrants have made new homes in squalid shantytowns. "I don't have papers," shrugs Alioune Soguie, a Senegalese man living in a shantytown near the Spanish city of Cádiz. "If I had papers, I wouldn't have to live like this."[53]

Many American immigration experts who have observed the situation in Spain have concluded that the liberal immigration policies now being reconsidered have not worked. Kitty Calavita, a University of California at Irvine professor who has studied international immigration laws, says that although liberal policies such as Spain's *regularización* program welcome illegal immigrants when the economy is booming, during down times these immigrants are treated like criminals and cannot afford decent housing. Moreover, the illegal immigrants find themselves hated by the host country's native residents. "The human toll is enormous," Calavita says, "with thousands of border crossing deaths every year, appalling living and working conditions for immigrants, and retaliation and civil rights violations by locals."[54]

The *Badanti* of Italy

Italy has similar problems to those of Spain—high unemployment as well as a geographic location that places the country within a short sea voyage of North Africa. As in Spain, the Italian coast guard patrols the waters off the country's southern coastline, intercepting boats and taking passengers into custody. In addition, Italian authorities have signed agreements with officials in the North African country of Libya, who have promised to police the country's coastline more closely, searching for boats embarking for Italy. (Spain has signed similar agreements with Senegal and Mauritania.) In other respects, however, Italy in the second decade of the twenty-first century has taken an even harder line against illegal immigration.

Italian officials realize their country faces a unique problem: Italy is plagued by the country's own demographics. It has one of the oldest populations, and one of the lowest birthrates, on earth. There have often been shortages of young Italians to fill jobs—particularly those held by the *badanti*, or caregivers to the elderly. In other words, there are simply not enough young Italians willing to accept the low pay that goes with the job of taking care of elderly Italians.

And so the Italian government has made a special exception for immigrants, including illegal immigrants, willing to accept jobs as *badanti*. A typical *badanta* is Olga Lukarch, who had worked as a highly paid engineer in Ukraine. When that country's economy collapsed in 2000 Lukarch lost her job. With no prospects at home, she traveled to Italy on a tourist visa, then stayed to look for work. Typically, tourist visas are granted for short periods—a few weeks or months at most. When she had overstayed the terms of her visa, Lukarch became an illegal immigrant in Italy.

Eventually, Lukarch found employment as a *badanta*. She moved into her employer's apartment, where she helps the older woman dress and cleans her home. Lukarch works six days a week and earns about $2,300 a month. "It's a very hard life,"[55] she says.

Lukarch did not face deportation. In 2002, two years after her visa had run out, Lukarch was granted amnesty by the Italian government. In America, many people who call for a tough policy against illegal immigrants readily acknowledge that many Mexicans and other Hispanic workers accept the type of jobs that Americans typically do not take: gardener, nanny and housekeeper, and day laborer, among others. In Italy, the hard-liners have embraced the idea that there are simply some jobs that many Italians are not inclined to accept, and so the immigration rules should be tailored to ensure that workers are found for these jobs. "Domestic work is the sector with the highest number of illegal immigrants," says Stephen Ogongo, a professor at the Pontifical Gregorian University in Rome. "Politicians . . . are fully aware of the important role immigrants, including the illegals, play in this society."[56]

> "In many ways, the crackdown in Italy mirrors the shift in the U.S., where mounting frustration over illegal immigration, partly fueled by the economic downturn, has led to increasingly tougher immigration laws at the local and state levels and record deportations at the federal level."[58]
>
> — American journalist Daniel González.

Crackdown in Italy

Although Italian political leaders have recognized the important role played by *badanti* in Italian society, the government still places strict rules on their status as legal visitors. Each caregiver must

The Mexican Border Fence

Inundated with as many as 500,000 illegal immigrants from countries in Central and South America, Mexico commenced erection of a fence along its southern border with Guatemala in 2010. Mexican officials have often voiced complaints about the border fence along the country's border with the United States, but they fiercely defend the need for their own fence along Mexico's southern border. "It could . . . prevent the free passage of illegal immigrants," insists Raúl Diaz, a tax administrator for the Mexican government.

Guatemalans and other people from Central and South America slip into Mexico for the same reason Mexicans and others cross illegally into the United States: they seek to escape poverty for opportunities elsewhere. In Chiapas, Mexico's southernmost state, Guatemalans are willing to work in farm fields for as little as $6 a day—a wage most Mexicans refuse to accept.

As is common elsewhere, illegal immigrants face hostility and danger as they enter Mexico. Men are frequently beaten, while women are often raped. "This society does not see migrants as human beings, it sees them as criminals," says Lucía del Carmen Bermúdez, coordinator for the Mexican government immigration agency Grupo Beta. "The majority of the attacks against migrants are not committed by authorities. . . . Most violence against migrants comes from civilians."

Quoted in *European Union Times*, "Mexico Is Now Building Their Own Wall On Border With Guatemala," September 19, 2010. www.eutimes.net.

Quoted in Ginger Thompson, "Mexico Worries About Its Own Southern Border," *New York Times*, June 18, 2006. www.nytimes.com.

apply for renewal of his or her visa annually. Moreover, every visa is immediately terminated upon the death of the employer—an understandably common occurrence. However, the government does give unemployed *bandati* opportunities to find other employers before they face deportation and, given the shortage of caregivers in Italy, most do find other jobs.

Other illegal immigrants in Italy are given far less friendly treatment. As the Italian economy soured, lawmakers approved new anti-immigration laws. One measure adopted in 2009 by the Italian parliament imposes penalties on people who provide homes for illegal immigrants. This measure is similar to the economic sanctions that American communities such as Hazleton, Pennsylvania, and Fremont, Nebraska, have tried to impose on landlords who rent apartments to illegal immigrants. Italy, however, has taken the measure a step further: a landlord who rents an apartment to an illegal immigrant faces time in jail. Indeed, Italian political leader Davide Cavallotto says that many of the new policies implemented in his country are based on the harshest anti-immigration laws passed in America, particularly those in Arizona. "We have a responsibility to protect and serve our own citizens,"[57] says Cavallotto.

Visitors to Rome can see this get-tough policy implemented on a regular basis. American journalist Daniel González, who witnessed Roman police officers chase down two street vendors they suspected of being illegal immigrants, writes:

> A few years ago, the police may never have bothered the men. But Italy has cracked down hard on illegal immigrants in recent years, adopting some of the strictest immigration-enforcement policies in Europe and deporting tens of thousands of people in the country illegally.
>
> . . . In many ways, the crackdown in Italy mirrors the shift in the U.S., where mounting frustration over illegal immigration, partly fueled by the economic downturn, has led to increasingly tougher immigration laws at the local and state levels and record deportations at the federal level.[58]

Two-Front War in Greece

The borders of Italy and Spain are most porous along their southern coastlines. Greece has faced a similar invasion of tiny boats ferrying illegal immigrants to its shores and, like Italy and

Spain, has dispatched its coast guard to search for the vessels. Unlike other European countries, though, Greece faces a two-front war when it comes to guarding its borders: many illegal immigrants try to enter the country through an overland route, finding places to cross into Greece along the country's common border with Turkey.

According to authorities of the European Union (EU)—the alliance of 27 European countries that provides for a common economy and currency for those nations—of the 106,000 illegal immigrants apprehended while trying to enter EU countries in 2009, 75 percent were detained along the Greece-Turkey border. Some of these immigrants are Africans who choose a lengthy overland route rather than direct sea voyages across the Mediterranean, but most of the illegal travelers start their journeys from countries in the Middle East.

EU officials acknowledge that the Greece-Turkey border is porous—thousands of illegal immigrants slip through each year. Upon reaching Greece, many of these newcomers go no further, preferring to find homes in Greece. It is estimated that the illegal immigrant population of Greece stands around 300,000.

This huge influx of illegal immigrants has placed an enormous burden on social services in Greece as well as on the country's economy, which, like the economies of other European nations, suffered during the economic recession of the 2000 decade. Says Christos Papoutsis, minister for public order in Greece, "Greek society has exceeded its limit in its capacity to accommodate illegal immigrants. This is the hard reality and we have an obligation to the Greek citizen to deal with it."[59]

"Greek society has exceeded its limit in its capacity to accommodate illegal immigrants. This is the hard reality and we have an obligation to the Greek citizen to deal with it."[59]

— Christos Papoutsis, minister for public order in Greece.

Greece's Border Fence

To help stem the flow of illegal immigrants, in 2011 Greek authorities proposed erection of a fence along the country's border with Turkey. The fence would run along an 8-mile section (13km) of the border; the remainder of Greece's 132-mile border (212km) with Turkey runs along the Evros River (in Turkey, it is known as the Meric River).

Therefore, unlike the fence that separates the US and Mexico, which only partially seals the border, the Greece-Turkey fence would run the entire length of the overland border between the two countries. (Greece also plans to step up coast guard patrols in the Evros River.) According to a statement by the Ministry of Public Order, "The fence in question is to act as a preventive measure to curb illegal immigration and will be constructed along the country's only overland border with Turkey."[60]

The proposed fence in Greece has fallen under severe criticism. Daniel Esdras, head of the Greek office for the immigration advocacy group International Organization for Migration, notes that immigrants try to enter Greece and other European countries for the same reason they try to enter the United States: they are fleeing poverty, hoping to find better lives elsewhere. Instead

Many illegal immigrants try to enter Greece by boat or overland from Turkey. Like other countries, Greece is cracking down on illegal immigration. A group of would-be immigrants awaits their fate at a Greek detention center in 2009.

of finding ways to keep them out, Esdras says, EU authorities should find ways to make them into productive European citizens. He continues:

> The idea of building more walls around a Fortress Europe is outdated. These are not just Greece's borders, but also those of the European Union. And people will carry on trying to reach a better life unless conditions in their home countries are improved. This is something governments should together be focusing on.[61]

The Role of Frontex

The European Union has, nevertheless, endorsed the wall. Said EU spokesperson Michele Cercone, "It is important that these borders . . . are managed in order to discourage and interrupt traffickers and smugglers that exploit [illegal immigrants]."[62] Turkish officials have also supported erection of the fence and have pledged to do more to detain illegal immigrants who are making their way across Turkey.

In endorsing the fence, the EU said it has recently taken other steps to enhance border security among its member nations. In 2005 the EU created a new agency, Frontex, to help the 27 EU nations coordinate their border security plans. Each member nation still patrols its own borders, but since most EU states border either non-EU nations or open waters, the international organization recognized the need for cooperation.

Frontex has headed cooperative ventures among EU member nations designed to halt border crossings and coastal landings. For example, soon after the formation of Frontex in 2006, the agency organized Operation Hera. Over the course of three months, patrol boats, airplanes, and helicopters from Spain, Portugal, Italy, and Finland patrolled the Atlantic Ocean near the coasts of Senegal and Mauritania. Those two countries in West Africa are regarded as main launching points for boats carrying people illegally into Europe. Many of these boats head for the Canary Islands, which are off the African coast but under the governance of Spain.

Frontex coordinated the patrols by the aircraft and vessels supplied by the four participating countries, while also obtaining permission from Senegal and Mauritania to patrol their coastlines. In addition, immigration officers from Italy, France, Germany, and Portugal were assigned to detention centers in the Canary Islands where they identified the immigrants and made arrangements to return them to their home countries.

Most of the boats seized in Operation Hera were *cayucos,* which are Senegalese fishing boats. Over the course of three months, the participants in Operation Hera detained *cayucos* carrying 1,243 illegal immigrants. "That's 1,243 who have not got to the Canaries," says Eduardo Lobo, a Spanish coast guard commander. "It is a preventative operation. If we locate and identify any illegal boat within 24 miles of the coast they are immediately returned."[63]

Desperate People

Clearly, countries in Europe have taken a number of measures to either stem the flow of illegal immigrants across their borders or, in some cases, find ways to legalize the presence of those who have made it across their borders. Spain maintained a very liberal immigration policy until the country's economy could no longer support great numbers of illegal visitors. Italy has also begun turning away illegal immigrants but has made exceptions for the *badanti,* who are workers the country desperately needs. Greek officials now intend to erect a border fence and, like the political leaders in America who have also endorsed a border fence, hear opposition from those who question whether a physical barrier truly represents a humanitarian strategy.

Indeed, many illegal immigrants have died in the Arizona desert, searching for ways to enter the United States, and yet many others are willing to risk their lives by making similar treks across the desert. Judging by the number of immigrants who have drowned when their boats capsize in the Mediterranean Sea, it is clear that no matter what country they may call home, when people are desperate they will risk their lives to find new opportunities.

"And people will carry on trying to reach a better life unless conditions in their home countries are improved."[61]

— Daniel Esdras, head of the Greek office for the immigration advocacy group International Organization for Migration.

Facts

- In 2009 the Italian government authorized an amnesty granting legal status to 600,000 *badanti* who had been living in the country illegally.

- To help secure their borders, the 27 nations of the European Union employ some 400,000 Border Patrol officers.

- Frontex officials have estimated that as many as 2,000 illegal immigrants drown each year when their tiny boats capsize in the Atlantic Ocean between Senegal and the Canary Islands.

- According to Gokhan Sozer, the governor of the Turkish province of Edirne, the Meric River is so low in the summer that immigrants can easily avoid the Greek border fence and walk across the waterway into Greece.

- The typical Senegalese cayuco is about 100 feet (30m) long and can carry as many as 150 men, women, and children crammed side by side for the eight to ten days it takes the boats to reach the Canary Islands.

- According to Frontex, 90 percent of illegal immigrants living in the European Union have gained access to the EU through Greece.

- Under rules adopted by the European Union nations in 2008, illegal immigrants can be held in detention centers for up to 18 months; after deportation, they are barred from entering an EU country, even legally, for five years.

Should Congress Enact a Path to Citizenship?

In 2009 nearly 750,000 foreign-born residents of America became naturalized citizens of the United States. Application for citizenship is the first step on this path. Next, most immigrants must undergo a lengthy process that includes continuous and law-abiding residency in America for at least five years, as well as proof of some ability to communicate in English and an understanding of US history and government, and the principles of democracy.

Many advocates believe that, rather than expending billions of dollars on a border fence or chasing down and deporting illegal immigrants who are already in America, it would be much more prudent to make them into citizens. This "path to citizenship" was first proposed in 2006 by President George W. Bush, who suggested that if illegal immigrants have held jobs for a number of years, and have broken no laws, they should be granted legal residency status and placed on track to become citizens:

> I believe that illegal immigrants who have roots in our country and want to stay should have to pay a meaningful penalty for breaking the law: to pay their taxes, to learn English, and to work in a job for a number of years. People who meet these conditions should be able to apply for citizenship but approval would not be automatic, and they will have to wait in line behind those who played by

the rules and followed the law. What I have just described is not amnesty—it is a way for those who have broken the law to pay their debt to society, and demonstrate the character that makes a good citizen.[64]

Playing by the Rules

Bush's proposal failed to gain traction in Congress. Conservative members, mostly from the border states, blocked the president's initiative and the idea died. One opponent, Representative Lamar Smith of Texas, suggested that Bush's proposal would, in fact, be an amnesty because it would grant citizenship to lawbreakers. Smith has said that he does not oppose immigration—he believes there is a place for legal immigration in this country because legal immigrants bring diversity to American society as well as skills to the American workplace that add to the country's economic prosperity. However, he says, as well:

> Legal immigrants play by the rules, wait their turn and are invited. Others cut in front of the line, break our laws and enter illegally. Some people say that we need to pass a comprehensive immigration reform bill that includes amnesty for millions of illegal immigrants in the U.S. But citizenship is the greatest honor our country can bestow. It shouldn't be sold to lawbreakers for the price of a fine.[65]

Despite the opposition from Smith and other border state lawmakers, polls show that a majority of Americans support a path to citizenship for the type of illegal immigrants described by Bush—those who have been steady and consistent workers and have obeyed the law while living in America. Indeed, a 2010 poll commissioned by CNN found that a clear majority of Americans—some 81 percent—favor a path to citizenship for illegal immigrants.

Caravan of Buses

Proponents of providing a path to citizenship argue that the alternative solution to illegal immigration—tracking down some 11 million illegal residents of America and deporting them to their

home countries—is simply not a viable strategy. "Deporting [11] million people would require a caravan of buses stretching from San Diego to Alaska,"[66] says Marc R. Rosenblum, a professor of political science at the University of New Orleans and former staff member of the US Senate Subcommittee on Immigration. Moreover, Rosenblum says, the total cost of deporting 11 million immigrants has been estimated to cost some $240 billion. "This leaves legalization as the only practical solution,"[67] Rosenblum says.

If these immigrants were offered a path to citizenship, Rosenblum adds, they would be required to pay taxes and be less likely to be abused by unscrupulous employers—those who would pay them less than the federally mandated minimum wage, which stood at $7.25 an hour in 2011. In addition, he says, the illegal trade of smuggling immigrants to America would virtually dry up.

Bruce Fein, a former member of a US Department of Justice task force on illegal immigration, counters that suddenly providing legal status to 11 million illegal immigrants would not make the problem of illegal immigration go away. He predicts that these

Newly naturalized US citizens take the oath of allegiance in Philadelphia. Thousands of legal immigrants become US citizens each year but only after a lengthy wait and demonstrating a basic understanding of English, of US history and government, and of the principles of democracy.

former illegal immigrants would soon be replaced by millions more who would also expect to be given legal residency status and placed on a path to citizenship. "To be sure, legalization would benefit those who were formerly illegal, hike their tax payments, and reduce their vulnerability to exploitation by the unscrupulous," says Fein. "Sensible analysis, however, cannot stop there. Legalization would also fuel more illegal migration, and compound the problem."[68]

Bipartisan Plan

Although Bush's path to citizenship plan failed to garner support in Congress, President Barack Obama attempted to revive the concept in 2010, backing the bipartisan bill of Senators Schumer of New York and Graham of South Carolina. The bill proposed by the New York Democrat and the South Carolina Republican incorporated Bush's basic notion of establishing a path to citizenship but also required illegal immigrants to admit to having broken the law, to pay a fine as well as back taxes, to pass background checks to ensure they are not wanted for crimes, and to prove they can speak English. Under the Schumer-Graham bill, if the illegal immigrants comply with all those requirements, they would be awarded places in line for naturalization behind those who have entered the country legally.

President Obama has put forth his position: "What has become increasingly clear is that we can no longer wait to fix our broken immigration system, which Democrats and Republicans alike agree doesn't work. It's unacceptable to have 11 million people in the United States who are living here illegally and outside of the system."[69] Obama has said that while he favors strict measures to control security at the border, he also favors a path to citizenship for those already in the country: "[That path] must require those who are here illegally to get right with the law, pay penalties and taxes, learn English, pass criminal background checks and admit responsibility before they are allowed to get in line and eventually earn citizenship."[70]

"I believe that illegal immigrants who have roots in our country and want to stay should have to pay a meaningful penalty for breaking the law: to pay their taxes, to learn English, and to work in a job for a number of years. People who meet these conditions should be able to apply for citizenship."[64]

— George W. Bush, forty-third president of the United States.

Winning Legal Status

Although illegal immigrants often face deportation if they step forward and identify themselves, there are some ways in which they can win legal status and remain in America. Many people who escape from repressive or dictatorial regimes can apply for political asylum once arriving in America. Since the early 1960s, the US government has welcomed many Cubans who have fled the regime of dictator Fidel Castro (and more recently Raúl Castro), granting them legal residency status.

Others who have resided in America illegally for more than 10 years can apply for "cancellation of removal" status. To qualify, the illegal immigrant must prove that a spouse, parent, or child is a citizen of the United States. However, in these cases, approval is not automatic. The applicant must prove to US Citizenship and Immigration Services that he or she would suffer an "exceptional and extremely serious hardship" if forced to leave America.

A final strategy is to convince a member of Congress to intervene. Immigration officials have granted legal status to illegal immigrants who are backed by members of Congress, usually on humanitarian grounds. Otherwise, to obtain legal status, immigration officials counsel most illegal immigrants to return to their home countries and then apply for visas to enter America legally.

Quoted in National Immigration Law Center, "Immigration Law and Policy: Removal Procedures and Defenses," 2001. www.nilc.org.

As before, border state lawmakers bristled at the plan and vowed to defeat it. "We could cut unemployment in half simply by reclaiming the jobs taken by illegal workers," complains Smith, the Texas Republican. "President Obama is on the wrong side of the American people on immigration. The president should support policies that help citizens and legal immigrants find the jobs they need and deserve, rather than fail to enforce immigration laws."[71] Meanwhile, in the Senate, Republican John Kyl of Arizona says, "All Americans would be better served if this administration focused on implementing proven border security solutions."[72]

The DREAM Act

While Congress has failed to adopt comprehensive plans mapping out a path to citizenship, lawmakers have examined other measures that would help selected illegal immigrants obtain legal status and eventually citizenship. One measure that gained considerable support in Washington, DC, was the proposed Development, Relief and Education of Alien Minors (DREAM) Act, which was designed to grant legal status to hundreds of thousands of young people who were brought to the country illegally by their parents. The beneficiaries of the act would be immigrants who as babies or young children were smuggled across the border by their parents.

"We were children when we came here," says Maria Marroquin, a 23-year-old resident of Philadelphia. "We had no choice. We didn't make the decision. Since arriving we did everything that was asked of us. We are American in every way."[73]

Marroquin and her parents are from Peru. She was 13 years old when she accompanied her parents on a trip to America. Her parents overstayed their visas, becoming illegal residents. In the 10 years after her arrival in America, Marroquin graduated from high school and earned an associate's degree from a community college, graduating with a grade point average of 3.98. As an illegal immigrant, though, Marroquin has been unable to obtain a Social Security number and, therefore, she cannot find full-time employment. The only positions that have been open to her have been temporary babysitting jobs.

> "Legalization would benefit those who were formerly illegal, hike their tax payments, and reduce their vulnerability to exploitation by the unscrupulous. . . . Legalization would also fuel more illegal migration, and compound the problem."[68]
>
> — Bruce Fein, a former member of a US Department of Justice task force on illegal immigration.

Minor Step

Under the DREAM Act, young people brought to the country before the age of 16 could attain legal residency status if they finished high school or earned a general educational development (GED) diploma, and then entered college or the military. Marroquin says that if the DREAM Act is adopted, she will return to college to earn a bachelor's degree. She also hopes to go to law school. "We're not asking for amnesty," says Marroquin, "just the chance to be legal and contribute to our country."[74]

The DREAM Act has faced considerable opposition. Border state lawmakers complained that the measure simply represents a minor step toward immigration reform and does not address the issue they consider paramount in the debate: the porous border between Mexico and America. Says Senator John Cornyn, a Republican from Texas:

> We have to demonstrate that we are serious about fixing our broken immigration system, we have to secure the border, we have to enforce our laws, and then I think the natural compassion of the American people will kick in, and they'll let us deal with these sympathetic situations like these kids who . . . were brought here by their parents and find themselves at a dead end."[75]

In 2010 the DREAM Act passed in the House but failed in the Senate by a close vote. In the election held a few months after the DREAM Act vote, Republican candidates—many of whom favor stricter measures to control illegal immigration—captured many seats in Congress. The sweeping victory by the Republicans gave them a majority in the House. The Democrats maintained control of the Senate, but their majority in that body decreased. Generally, Democrats have been more open to liberalizing immigration laws. Because of the increased influence of Republican lawmakers in Washington, the future of measures such as the DREAM Act remains very much in doubt.

Still, the DREAM Act continues to find many supporters in the nation's capital and elsewhere. Says Senator Robert Menendez, a Democrat from New Jersey, "I believe we are still a nation that would rather welcome our promising and patriotic youth with a warm embrace rather than a cold shoulder because of their parents' actions. [The Senate] vote will not soon be forgotten by a community that is growing in size, but also in

"We could cut unemployment in half simply by reclaiming the jobs taken by illegal workers."[71]

— US representative Lamar Smith, a Republican from Texas.

Students in Phoenix, Arizona, march in support of the DREAM Act, a proposed federal law that would grant legal status to young people who were brought into the United States illegally by their parents. Efforts to pass the law failed in 2010.

power and political awareness."[76] Adds Alicia Cortes, 19, who was born in Mexico and entered America illegally as a young child, "They did not defeat us, they ignited our fire."[77]

The *Dred Scott* Decision

As a result of the failure of the DREAM Act to garner enough votes for adoption, anti-immigration advocates suggested that instead of finding ways to make it easier for illegal immigrants to attain legal status and eventually become citizens, existing citizenship laws should be reexamined and made stricter. Specifically, these advocates have called for repeal of the 14th Amendment to the Constitution.

The intent of the post–Civil War amendment, which grants citizenship to all children born in America, was to resolve the issues of citizenship for former slaves. Captured in Africa and brought to America by slave traders, these people, or their children and grandchildren, were emancipated during the Civil War but had been denied citizenship by a decision handed down by the Supreme Court in 1857. That decision, in the infamous *Dred Scott* case, held that neither freed slaves nor their descendants could ever become citizens because they had been the properties of others. (Scott was a slave who sued for his freedom; the Supreme Court ruled that since he was not a citizen, he had no right to sue his owner in the courts.)

Anchor Babies

The Fourteenth Amendment negated the *Dred Scott* decision, making it clear that people born in America, regardless of the citizenship status of their parents, are American citizens. Section 1 of the amendment begins: "All persons born or naturalized in the United States are citizens of the United States and of the State wherein they reside."

Although that language would appear to put an end to the argument, anti-immigration advocates suggest that the Constitution should be changed. They argue for repealing the Fourteenth Amendment, since some babies born in America have parents who entered the country illegally. They contend that illegal immigrants have found ways to exploit the law to their advantage, suggesting that some pregnant women enter the country illegally for the purpose of giving birth to "anchor babies." Since these babies are citizens, the government cannot deport them, virtually guaranteeing to their mothers permission to remain as well. "[Thousands] of illegal aliens are crossing U.S. borders to give birth and exploit their child as an 'anchor baby' to obtain residency and other benefits for themselves,"[78] insists Daryl Metcalfe, a state legislator from Pennsylvania and leader of the national group State Legislators for Legal Immigration.

> "[Thousands] of illegal aliens are crossing U.S. borders to give birth and exploit their child as an 'anchor baby' to obtain residency and other benefits for themselves."[78]
>
> — Daryl Metcalfe, a state legislator from Pennsylvania and leader of State Legislators for Legal Immigration.

Defending the Fourteenth Amendment

Critics like Metcalfe believe that birth statistics support their claims. Indeed, a study by the Pew Hispanic Center found that 8 percent of the 4.3 million babies born in America in 2008—in other words, nearly 350,000 babies—had at least one parent living in the country illegally. "Women have traveled from across the world for the purpose of adding a U.S. passport holder to their family, as far away as China, Turkey, and as close as Mexico,"[79] says Jon Feere, a legal analyst for the Center for Immigration

Should Illegal Immigrants Serve in the American Military?

The first American soldier to lose his life in the Iraq War was Jose Gutierrez, a marine corporal who died on March 23, 2003. Gutierrez, a native of Guatemala, entered America illegally when he was 14. An orphan, Gutierrez was eventually granted legal residency on humanitarian grounds. After winning his green card, Gutierrez enlisted in the marines.

Noncitizens who are legal residents of America are permitted to enlist in the armed forces. Many enlist because they are permitted to apply for citizenship as soon as they enter the service. About 35,000 foreign citizens are currently members of the American armed forces; about 8,500 enlist every year.

The armed forces do not accept illegal immigrants, but many advocates believe that policy should change—that illegal immigrants who enlist should be granted legal residency status and put on a path to citizenship. The proposed DREAM Act included a provision enabling young illegal immigrants to gain legal status by enlisting in the military. According to Senator Richard Durbin, Democrat of Illinois, "The Army is struggling to meets its recruitment goals. Under the DREAM Act, tens of thousands of well-qualified potential recruits would become eligible for military service for the first time. They are eager to serve in the armed forces during a time of war." In the final vote in 2010, however, the measure was defeated in the Senate.

Quoted in Rick Maze, "Bill Would Grant Citizenship for Service," *Army Times*, July 16, 2007. www.armytimes.com.

Studies, a Washington, DC–based group that favors strict immigration laws.

Nevertheless, the Fourteenth Amendment has many defenders who argue that changing the Constitution would not stem the flow of illegal immigration into America. They insist that American citizenship is not the primary motivation that drives people to slip across the border—it is the opportunity to escape the poverty of Mexico and other countries in search of better living standards. Douglas Massey, a Princeton University demographer who has studied immigration issues for 30 years, says he has never interviewed an immigrant who claimed to have entered the country illegally to give birth to a baby so she could remain. "Mexicans do not come to have babies in the United States," he says. "They end up having babies in the United States because men can no longer circulate freely back and forth from homes in Mexico to jobs in the United States, and husbands and wives quite understandably want to be together."[80]

Moreover, repealing the Fourteenth Amendment could also mean denying citizenship to children born to parents who have entered the country legally. Many of these children have gone on to become productive contributors to American society. Among them are the actress Renée Zellweger, a native of Texas whose foreign-born parents (from Switzerland and Norway) had entered the country legally. Also, baseball star Alex Rodriguez is the son of two legal immigrants from the Dominican Republic—he was born in New York City shortly after his parents moved to America.

Politically Charged Atmosphere

Prospects for repealing the Fourteenth Amendment are remote. Amending the Constitution is a lengthy process. A bill to repeal an amendment, must pass both houses of Congress by majorities of at least two-thirds. Next, the measure must be approved by at least three-quarters of the states—processes that are usually resolved through votes by the state legislatures. Typically, a sunset provision of seven years is included in the legislation passed by Congress—meaning that if the measure is not approved by three-fourths of the states within seven years, the move to repeal dies.

In fact, since ratification of the Constitution more than 200 years ago, only one amendment has been repealed; it was the 18th Amendment, which outlawed the sale of alcoholic beverages in America, creating the era of Prohibition. After a disastrous period of American history in which it became clear that enforcing Prohibition was impossible, the 18th Amendment was repealed in its entirety after a mere 13 years as law.

Given the politically charged atmosphere as well as the divisive feelings regarding illegal immigration, it would seem that the movement to repeal the Fourteenth Amendment lacks the overwhelming public support often required to ensure revision of the Constitution. A poll commissioned by CNN in early 2011 found Americans in sharp division over the question—51 percent opposed repeal, while 49 percent favored denying citizenship to the American-born children of immigrants—both legal and illegal. "Repeal would be . . . short-sighted," says Alan Jenkins, executive director of the New York–based civil rights group Opportunity Agenda. "It would allow the rancorous politics of the moment to deny a core constitutional freedom to 300 million Americans citizens. It would carve a single group of people—babies no less—out of a guarantee that was rightly granted to all of us."[81]

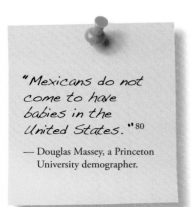

"Mexicans do not come to have babies in the United States."[80]
— Douglas Massey, a Princeton University demographer.

An Effective Strategy

As the divisiveness over the proposed repeal of the Fourteenth Amendment indicates, there has never been an easy solution to stemming the flow of illegal immigration into America. Despite a century of devising laws to control immigration, people continue to flock across borders illegally, seeking better opportunities in America. Other countries, including Spain, Italy, and Greece, face similar pressures and, like America, have been unable to find ways to seal their borders while still maintaining the concept that free societies should welcome the oppressed and underprivileged.

The ultimate solution to reducing the flow of illegal immigrants would seem to hinge on improving people's lives in their own countries. But while America can provide foreign aid and send Peace Corps volunteers into impoverished countries, the quality of life in those countries is largely under the control of the national and local leaders.

Therefore, lawmakers in America are instead searching for ways to secure the country's borders while crafting policies to address the status of the people who are already here illegally. In recent years, all manner of solutions have been proposed and implemented: erection of a border fence, deportation of illegal immigrants, amnesties, and a proposed path to citizenship are all part of the mix. All of these tactics have found opposition among segments of the American public. It would seem, then, that until the nation can unite behind an effective strategy, people from foreign countries will continue to find ways to slip across the border in search of greater possibilities for themselves and their families.

Facts

- If the DREAM Act had passed Congress in 2010, it would have granted legal status to 825,000 immigrants brought illegally to America by their parents, according to the Washington, DC–based Migration Policy Institute.

- According to a report cited by the Council on Foreign Relations, a Washington, DC–based research organization, 90 percent of legal immigrants pay federal taxes while just 60 percent of illegal immigrants pay federal taxes.

- A study by the Pew Hispanic Center found that of the 340,000 babies born to illegal immigrants in 2008, 85 percent of the parents had been in America for more than a year, and more than 50 percent of the parents had been in America for more than five years.

- Members of Congress have introduced legislation to repeal the Fourteenth Amendment three times since 2005; none of those bills made it to the floors of the House or Senate for full votes.

- A 2010 poll sponsored by the CBS television network reported that 68 percent of Americans favor adoption of the DREAM Act; the poll also reported support for the bill among 88 percent of Hispanic Americans.

Related Organizations and Websites

American Immigration Council (AIC)

1331 G St. NW, Suite 200
Washington, DC 20005
phone: (202) 507-7500
fax: (202) 742-5619
website: www.americanimmigrationcouncil.org

AIC studies immigration issues and lobbies for laws that support the rights of immigrants. Students visiting the AIC website can find a defense of the Fourteenth Amendment, which includes essays by experts who contend that the provisions in the amendment's first sentence are not abused by illegal immigrants.

Federation for American Immigration Reform (FAIR)

25 Massachusetts Ave. NW, Suite 330
Washington, DC 20001
phone: (877) 627-3247
fax: (202) 387-3447
website: www.fairus.org

FAIR lobbies for laws that would impede the flow of illegal immigrants into America. Visitors to the FAIR website can find many studies and position papers drafted by the organization that support its claims that illegal immigrants threaten the security of Americans and drain society's resources for health care and education.

National Immigration Law Center (NILC)

3435 Wilshire Blvd., Suite 2850
Los Angeles, CA 90010
phone: (213) 639-3900
fax: (213) 639-3911
e-mail: info@nilc.org
website: www.nilc.org

NILC lobbies for laws protecting immigrants' rights and seeks court actions overturning measures it believes infringe on the rights of immigrants. Visitors to the NILC website can find the organization's position on measures that individual states have enacted to make it more difficult for illegal immigrants to obtain driver's licenses.

Pew Hispanic Center

1615 L St. NW, Suite 700
Washington, DC 20036
phone: (202) 419-3600
fax: (202) 419-3608
e-mail: info@pewhispanic.org
website: http://pewhispanic.org

The Pew Hispanic Center researches many issues with the goal of increasing the understanding of the Hispanic American community. Studies about illegal immigration can be accessed on the organization's website, including reports on Arizona's immigration law and studies of the declining illegal immigration population in America.

US Citizenship and Immigration Services (CIS)

20 Massachusetts Ave. NW
Washington, DC 20529
phone: (202) 272-1200
website: www.uscis.gov

Foreign citizens who wish to obtain visas to visit America either for brief or extended periods must apply through CIS. The agency also administers the naturalization program for immigrants who seek American citizenship. By visiting the agency's website, students can learn about the rules foreign citizens must follow to obtain naturalization.

US Customs and Border Protection (CBP)

1300 Pennsylvania Ave. NW
Washington, DC 20229
phone: (703) 526-4200
website: www.cbp.gov

An agency of the US Department of Homeland Security, CBP is responsible for ensuring the country's borders are secure. The agency includes the US Border Patrol. Visitors to the CBP website can find many details about the Border Patrol's mission, including how units are deployed and how officers conduct searches at points of entry.

US Immigration and Customs Enforcement (ICE)

500 12th St. SW
Washington, DC 20536
phone: (202) 732-4242
website: www.ice.gov

ICE investigates cases of human trafficking in which "coyotes" smuggle illegal immigrants into the country. ICE agents also conduct workplace raids on farm fields and in sweatshop factories. By accessing the Image and Video Gallery on the ICE website, students can view footage of actual ICE operations.

Additional Reading

Books

Tim Gaynor, *Midnight on the Line: The Secret Life of the US-Mexico Border*. New York: Thomas Dunne, 2009.

David Haugen, Susan Musser, and Kacy Lovelace, eds., *At Issue: Should the US Close Its Borders?* Farmington Hills, MI: Greenhaven Press, 2010.

Noël Merino, ed., *At Issue: What Rights Should Illegal Immigrants Have?* Farmington Hills, MI: Greenhaven Press, 2010.

Johnny Rico, *Border Crosser: One Gringo's Illicit Passage from Mexico into America*. New York: Ballantine, 2009.

Terry Green Sterling, *Illegal: Life and Death in Arizona's Immigration War Zone*. Guilford, CT: Lyons Press, 2010.

Periodicals

Arian Campo-Flores, "Will Arizona's New Immigration Law Lead to Racial Profiling?," *Newsweek*, April 27, 2010.

Claudia Dreifus, "A Surgeon's Path from Migrant Fields to Operating Room," *New York Times*, May 13, 2008.

Dan Nowicki, "Arizona's Immigration Law Ripples Through History, US Politics," *Arizona Republic*, July 25, 2010.

Nathan Thornburgh, "The Battle for Arizona," *Time*, June 14, 2010.

Daniel B. Wood, "Along US-Mexican Border, an Erratic Patchwork Fence," *Christian Science Monitor*, April 3, 2008.

Internet Sources

Arizona Republic, "Crossings: A Planet on the Move." www.azcentral.com/news/global-immigration.

CBS *60 Minutes*, "Welcome to Hazleton: One Mayor's Controversial Plan to Deal with Illegal Immigration." www.cbsnews.com/stories/2006/11/17/60minutes/main2195789.shtml.

PBS.com, *The Border*. www.pbs.org/kpbs/theborder/index.html.

PBS.com, *The Border Fence*. www.pbs.org/now/shows/432.

Time, "The New Frontier." www.time.com/time/covers/1101010611/fcities.html.

Source Notes

Introduction: A Country Divided

1. Quoted in David Dudley, "The Alfredo Story," *Hopkins Medicine*, Winter 2007. www.hopkinsmedicine.org.
2. Quoted in Max Alexander, "An Illegal Immigrant Turned Brain Surgeon—with His Own Two Hands," *Readers Digest*, February 2008. www.rd.com.
3. Quoted in Charisse Jones, "States Torn on Illegals' Rights," *USA Today*, May 1, 2005. www.usatoday.com.
4. Sam Francis, "Troops on the Border," November 14, 2002. www.vdare.com.
5. David DeCosse, "Can Citizenship Be Earned?," *America*, October 13, 2008. www.americamagazine.org.
6. Quoted in Claudia Dreifus, "A Surgeon's Path from Migrant Fields to Operating Room," *New York Times*, May 13, 2008. www.nytimes.com.

Chapter One: What Are the Roots of the Controversy over Illegal Immigration?

7. Quoted in Randal C. Archibold, "Ranchers Alarmed by Killing Near Border," *New York Times*, April 5, 2010, p. A-9.
8. Quoted in Archibold, "Ranchers Alarmed by Killing Near Border," p. A-9.
9. Quoted in Keith Phucas, "DA: Cocaine Trail Leads to Mexican Drug Cartel," *Norristown (PA) Times Herald*, December 16, 2010. www.timesherald.com.
10. Quoted in Will Weissert, Associated Press, "Countless Juárez Residents Flee 'Dying City,'" Yahoo! News, December 29, 2010. http://news.yahoo.com.
11. Federation for American Immigration Reform, *The Sinking Lifeboat: Uncontrolled Immigration and the US Health Care System*, February 2004. www.fairus.org.

12. Quoted in Jeff Chirico, "Study Argues Immigration Creates More Jobs for Americans," *CBS Atlanta*, November 1, 2010. www.cbsatlanta.com.

13. Quoted in Allen Jayne, *Jefferson's Declaration of Independence: Origins, Philosophy, and Theology.* Lexington: University of Kentucky Press, 1998, p. 54.

Chapter Two: Can America Effectively Seal Its Borders?

14. Quoted in John King, "Border Fence Is a Dividing Line in Immigration Debate," CNN, February 13, 2009. www.cnn.com.

15. Quoted in NOW, "The Border Fence," August 15, 2008. www.pbs.org.

16. Quoted in *Political Transcripts*, "US Senators Patrick Leahy and Arlen Specter Hold a News Conference on the Immigration Substitute Legislation," March 30, 2006.

17. Quoted in Howard LeFranchi, "America Puts Up Chain-Links Along a Once-Friendly Border," *Christian Science Monitor*, February 13, 1996, p. 9.

18. Quoted in Daniel B. Wood, "Along US-Mexican Border, an Erratic Patchwork Fence," *Christian Science Monitor*, April 3, 2008. www.csmonitor.com.

19. Duncan Hunter, "If We Build It They Won't Come," *Human Events*, May 22, 2007. www.humanevents.com.

20. Quoted in King, "Border Fence Is a Dividing Line in Immigration Debate."

21. Quoted in Terry McCarthy, "The Coyote's Game," *Time*, June 11, 2001, p. 56.

22. Quoted in McCarthy, "The Coyote's Game," p. 56.

23. Quoted in NOW, "Issue Clash: Illegal Immigration," March 25, 2009. www.pbs.org.

24. Quoted in Griselda Nevarez, "Many Illegal Immigrants Overstay Visas," *Yuma (AZ) Sun*, September 20, 2010. www.yumasun.com.

25. Chris Liska Carger, *Dreams Deferred: Dropping Out and Struggling Forward.* Charlotte, NC: Information Age, 2009, p. 2.

26. Quoted in Lourdes Medrano, "Border Deaths for Illegal Immigrants Hit Record High in Arizona Sector," *Christian Science Monitor*, December 16, 2010. www.csmonitor.com.

27. Quoted in King, "Border Fence Is a Dividing Line in Immigration Debate."

28. Tom Tancredo, "No Fence, No Border? No Bull," *Human Events*, May 28, 2008. www.humanevents.com.

29. Quoted in Emma Perez-Trevino, "Costly Efforts to Secure Border Not Paying Off," *Brownsville (TX) Herald*, June 20, 2010. www.brownsvilleherald.com.

30. Quoted in Suzanne Gamboa, "Guard Troops Head to Border Aug. 1," *Philadelphia Inquirer*, July 20, 2010, p. A3.

31. Quoted in Nina Bernstein, "Border Sweeps in North Reach Miles into US," *New York Times*, August 30, 2010, p. A1.

32. Quoted in David Kravets, "Lawmakers Eyeing National ID Card," *Wired*, March 23, 2010. www.wired.com.

33. American Civil Liberties Union, "Five Problems with National Identity Cards," September 8, 2003. www.aclu.org.

34. Quoted in Wood, "Along US-Mexican Border, an Erratic Patchwork Fence."

35. Quoted in Gamboa, "Guard Troops Head to Border Aug. 1," p. A3.

Chapter Three: Can Illegal Immigration Be Policed Within US Borders?

36. Quoted in *CBS News*, "Welcome to Hazleton: One Mayor's Controversial Plan to Deal with Illegal Immigration," November 19, 2006. www.cbsnews.com.

37. Quoted in CNN, "Nebraska Immigration Law Passes," June 22, 2010. http://articles.cnn.com.

38. Quoted in *CBS News*, "Welcome to Hazleton: One Mayor's Controversial Plan to Deal with Illegal Immigration."

39. Quoted in Timberly Ross, "Town Votes to Ban Hiring, Renting to Illegal Immigrants," *Doylestown (PA) Intelligencer*, June 22, 2010, p. A4.

40. Quoted in Larry King, "Hazleton Law Loses Again in Courts," *Philadelphia Inquirer*, September 10, 2010, p. B1.

41. Quoted in *Delaware Online*, "Immigrant Bashing Pennsylvania Mayor Off to Congress," December 15, 2010. www.delaware online.com.

42. Quoted in Brady McCombs, "Focus in Krentz Killing on Suspect in US," *Arizona Daily Star*, May 3, 2010. http://azstarnet.com.

43. Quoted in Arian Campo-Flores, "Will Arizona's New Immigration Law Lead to Racial Profiling?," *Newsweek*, April 27, 2010. www.newsweek.com.

44. Quoted in Kasie Hunt, "Democrat: Arizona Law Like 'Nazi Germany,'" *Politico*, April 26, 2010. www.politico.com.

45. David Frum, "In Defense of Arizona," *The Week*, April 28, 2010. http://theweek.com.

46. Quoted in David S. Savage, "US Suit Seeks to Block Arizona Law," *Philadelphia Inquirer*, July 7, 2010, p. A6.

47. Quoted in Savage, "US Suit Seeks to Block Arizona Law," p. A6.

48. Quoted in Emily Bazar, "More States to Deny Illegal Migrants Driver's Licenses," *USA Today*, January 29, 2008. www.usatoday.com.

49. Quoted in Jennifer Ludden, "Immigration Experts Predict Fewer Workplace Raids," NPR, December 2, 2008. www.npr.org.

Chapter Four: Can Other Countries Serve as Models for US Policies?

50. Quoted in Giles Tremlett, "Baby Born on Mediterranean Crossing Recovers in Spanish Hospital," *Guardian*, December 13, 2010. www.guardian.co.uk.

51. Quoted in Daniel González and Dan Nowicki, "A Planet on the Move," *Arizona Republic*, December 12, 2010, p. SP2.

52. Quoted in Daniel González, "Once Popular System Breaks Down," *Arizona Republic*, December 12, 2010, p. SP7.

53. Quoted in González, "Once Popular System Breaks Down," p. SP7.

54. Kitty Calavita, "The Persistent Gap in Immigration Law and Its Stubborn Failures," American Academy of Political and Social Science, June 1, 2010. www.aapss.org.

55. Quoted in Daniel González, "A Hard Life Far from Home and Family," *Arizona Republic*, December 12, 2010, p. SP11.

56. Stephen Ogongo, "All Illegal Immigrants with Jobs Can Potentially Be Regularized," *Africa News*, August 20, 2009. www.africa-news.eu.

57. Quoted in Daniel González, "Arizona Law Inspires Italian Politician," *Arizona Republic*, December 12, 2010, p. SP10.

58. Daniel González, "Questions Amid a Crackdown," *Arizona Republic*, December 12, 2010, p. SP10.

59. Quoted in *BBC News*, "Greece Plans Turkey Border Fence to Tackle Migration," January 4, 2011. www.bbc.co.uk.

60. Quoted in Elinda Labropoulou, "Concern over Proposed Greek Border Fence," CNN, January 4, 2011. www.cnnstudentnews.cnn.com.

61. Quoted in Labropoulou, "Concern over Proposed Greek Border Fence."

62. Quoted in *BBC News*, "Greece Plans Turkey Border Fence to Tackle Migration."

63. Quoted in Dominic Bailey, "Stemming the Immigration Wave," *BBC News*, September 10, 2006. http://news.bbc.co.uk.

Chapter Five: Should Congress Enact a Path to Citizenship?

64. *New York Times*, "Transcript: Bush's Speech on Immigration," May 15, 2006. www.nytimes.com.

65. Quoted in John R. Parkinson, "Rupert Murdoch, Owner of Fox News, Argues for Immigration Reform," *ABC News*, September 30, 2010. http://blogs.abcnews.com.

66. Marc R. Rosenblum, in "A 'Path to Citizenship' for Current Illegal Immigrants?" Council on Foreign Relations, April 6, 2007. www.cfr.org.

67. Rosenblum, in "A 'Path to Citizenship' for Current Illegal Immigrants?"

68. Bruce Fein, in "A 'Path to Citizenship' for Current Illegal Immigrants?" Council on Foreign Relations, April 6, 2007. www.cfr.org.

69. The White House, *Statement by the President on Senate Proposal Outlined Today to Fix Our Nation's Broken Immigration System*, April 29, 2010. www.whitehouse.gov.

70. The White House, *Statement by the President on Senate Proposal Outlined Today to Fix Our Nation's Broken Immigration System*.

71. Quoted in Peter Baker, "Obama Prods Congress for Immigration Action," *Philadelphia Inquirer*, July 2, 2010, p. A16.

72. Quoted in Baker, "Obama Prods Congress for Immigration Action," p. A16.

73. Quoted in Michael Matza, "Seeking Votes for DREAM Act," *Philadelphia Inquirer*, December 1, 2010, p. B2.

74. Quoted in Matza, "Seeking Votes for DREAM Act," p. B2.

75. Quoted in Julie Hirschfeld Davis, "Senate Delays DREAM Act Vote, Short on Support for It," *Philadelphia Inquirer*, December 10, 2010, p. A7.

76. Quoted in Julia Preston, "DREAM Act Immigration Bill Falls Short in Senate," *Philadelphia Inquirer*, December 19, 2010, p. A4.

77. Quoted in Preston, "DREAM Act Immigration Bill Falls Short in Senate," p. A4.

78. Quoted in Michael Matza, "Pennsylvania Legislator in 'Birthright' Fight," *Philadelphia Inquirer*, January 6, 2011, p. B1.

79. Quoted in Bob Christie and Paul J. Weber, "Cross-Border Births Debated," *Philadelphia Inquirer*, September 5, 2010, p. A2.

80. Quoted in Bob Christie and Paul J. Weber, "Cross-Border Births Debated," p. A2.

81. Alan Jenkins, "Repealing the 14th Amendment Is Wrong for America," *The Hill*, August 9, 2010. http://thehill.com.

Index

Note: Boldface page numbers indicate illustrations.

About the Author

Hal Marcovitz is a former newspaper reporter and columnist and author of more than 150 books for young readers. His other titles in the *In Controversy* series include *How Serious a Threat Is Climate Change?* and *Is Offshore Oil Drilling Worth the Risks?* He makes his home in Chalfont, Pennsylvania.